Tree Surgery

1 Specimen *Liriodendron tulipifera*, over 30m (100ft) high. No tree surgery has been required to date

Tree Surgery

P. H. Bridgeman, NDH, ND Arb

DAVID & CHARLES
NEWTON ABBOT   LONDON
NORTH POMFRET (VT)

To families in general and mine in
particular

ISBN 0 7153 7050 2
Library of Congress Catalog Card Number
75-31320

© P. H. Bridgeman, P. J. Jordan and D. Patch 1976

First published 1976
Second impression 1977
Third impression 1979
Fourth impression 1980

Printed in Great Britain
by Redwood Burn Limited
Trowbridge and Esher
for David & Charles (Publishers) Limited
Brunel House   Newton Abbot   Devon

Published in the United States of America
by David & Charles Inc
North Pomfret   Vermont 05053   USA

Contents

List of Illustrations

The diagrams were drawn by M. John Whitehead, ND Arb, who also took the photographs from which all the plates have been reproduced, with the exception of plates 23, 35, 42 and 43 which have been taken from photographs by Michaél Neale. Figures shown in the text in brackets are plate numbers.

Preface

Tree surgery has developed and expanded greatly in the last decade. This practical guide to the knowledge and equipment required and methods of operation attempts to give an up-to-date account of the modern industry. It is intended to be a manual for those practising, supervising or managing tree surgery operations, and for allied professionals and tree owners in general who wish to understand the principles of the operations so that they can intelligently employ others.

Tree surgery is, of course, essentially practical with a high degree of danger in many of the operations. It is not possible to acquire these skills from the written word alone. This book can act only as a guide, and the knowledge gained must be associated with supervised practical training.

To become a competent tree surgeon, a person should not only be able to climb, carry out the various operations and handle complex machinery and equipment but must also understand the principles of the structure and functions of woody plants and their predators and be familiar with the various means by which trees can become the subject of litigation. I am extremely grateful to my colleagues, Derek Patch for his contributing chapter on the law as it affects tree surgery and Pam Jordan for her chapter on tree growth. The effects of pests, diseases and other troubles have been referred to throughout the text but, as this subject is so well documented in specialist works, the recognition and control of the various pathogens has not been dealt with.

Introduction

Definition and Scope of Tree Surgery

Tree surgery is an aspect of arboriculture, which has been defined as the production, selection, planting, cultivation and maintenance of woody plants for amenity. By that definition, arboriculture must work in close co-operation with its allied professions of horticulture, forestry and landscape design, construction and maintenance. In urban areas there must also be liaison with developers, architects, planners and engineers, and in the country with farmers, countryside recreation staff and conservationists. The growing public awareness of the environment has been directed towards a greater concern for trees by their natural beauty and permanence and, more directly, by the ravages of Dutch elm disease and the encouragement of the Department of Environment's tree planting promotions. This has resulted in arboriculture being recognised as an industry and profession in its own right with the need for standards equal to that of its more established allied professions.

Tree surgery is one aspect of arboriculture that possibly requires more attention to standards than any other. There is a degree of opinion that defines tree surgeons as 'loppers' or 'butchers', and such people still exist. They do, however, rely on public ignorance and naïvety and it is not too optimistic to assume that this will change as tree owners – both public and private – become more informed. With tree legislation, training schemes, modern equipment and the British Standards Institution *Recommendations for Tree Work* all now available there is no excuse for public bodies to employ sub-standard operators.

There is also the accusation that tree surgery is inimical to wildlife conservation through the removal of dead wood and treatment of cavities in trees. If such work is carried out in woodlands where there is no public danger this is a perfectly justifiable statement. However, where trees are growing in public parks, urban areas and highways there is the overriding responsibility for public safety. In such public situations tree surgery operations can be not only aesthetically desirable but essential if owners are to face up to public responsibilities. Most tree surgery units, both public and private, are concerned not just with the preservation of old, over-mature trees, but with the shaping and training of developing trees and the selection and transplanting of trees to give continuity to the tree scene.

Developments in Arboriculture and Tree Surgery

Although trees have been cultured for amenity and commercial interests for many hundreds of years, it is only in comparatively recent times that arboriculture has been recognised as an industry and profession in its own right. Arboriculturists have, of course, existed for much longer, particularly in the wealth of arboreta, botanic gardens and private estates throughout the world. Wherever trees were grown for amenity and public interest there was the need for correct tree surgery practices. This work was often carried out by garden and forestry staff. Many sound basic skills were established with what appears today to be very primitive tools and safety equipment.

By the 1930s commercial companies were offering tree surgery services. Among the first were the English Tree Expert Company Ltd and the Chiltern Tree Surgeons. After the war the more familiar companies of Southern Tree Surgeons Ltd, Beechings of Ash Ltd, and in 1954 Honey Brothers Ltd emerged. Names like Jim Beeching, Bill Matthews, Tom Wilson and Peter and Tony Honey became synonymous with the highest standards of tree surgery. In local government departments the arboricultural activities were mainly controlled by the parks superintendent or borough engineer. A significant landmark in arboriculture was the appointment of Ted Storey as the first full-time Arboricultural Officer to the then London County Council.

In 1958 the Royal Forestry Society of England, Wales and Northern Ireland established examinations specifically in Arboriculture. The Certificate and in 1959 the Diploma (later to be called the National Diploma in Arboriculture) not only set standards of knowledge and competency in arboricultural practices but gave recognition to arboriculture as a separate profession, encouraging young people to study and specialise in this field. Hubert Taylor, the Chief Examiner, is undoubtedly the man best qualified to set and test these standards.

Although many organisations and societies had an interest in amenity trees, the need was felt for more specialist associations. In 1964 both the Arboricultural Association, formed mainly by publicly employed staff, and the Association of British Tree Surgeons and Arborists, representing the commercial companies, were inaugurated. The Arboricultural Association grew rapidly, established branches throughout the country, produced advisory leaflets and compiled a register of arboricultural consultants. Don Wells, the first Chairman and now Treasurer and Derek Honour, the Secretary for the first ten years, not only carried the main administrative functions but helped initiate and confirm arboriculture as a profession.

The Association of British Tree Surgeons and Arborists concentrated on improving standards by establishing an approved list of tree surgery contractors, and its Annual Conference became the main national arboricultural event of the year. For its first conference, the Association approached Merrist Wood Agricultural College and from this small beginning the need for a complete education and training structure emerged. At a later conference and in conjunction with the Arboricultural Association the whole question of education was debated. The outcome was the establishment of a Standing Committee on Arboricultural Education and Training, representing the major organisations and interests, to study and make recommendations on education and training (see Appendix). Both organisations were major contributors to the British Standards Institution *Recommendations for Tree Work* (1966).

In the early 1970s, Honey Bros Ltd established the first specialist tree surgery equipment sales service. This not only gave a sales service backed by proven experience with equipment and techniques, but was able to approach manufacturers to develop and improve tree surgery equipment.

At the Merrist Wood Conference in 1972 the subject of arboricultural research was discussed and a working party was established to consider and report on this vital topic.

The two organisations mentioned above had similar aims, objectives and interests and in 1974 they amalgamated as the Arboricultural Association (Incorporating the Association of British Tree Surgeons and Arborists).

In 1975 many of the county councils, London boroughs and larger district councils have arboricultural expertise within their establishment with direct labour forces or are employing commercial companies. With the effects of the establishment of larger district authorities after local government reorganisation, the greater public and professional awareness of the need for sound tree care, the increased interest in amenity and recreation by the Forestry and Countryside Commissions and commercial forestry and an established career and education structure, all augurs well for the future of arboriculture. The formation of the Tree Council, representing all aspects of tree care and land use and with government support, should provide adequate safeguards and co-ordination of effort to ensure this promising future.

1 Tree Growth
P. J. Jordan, MI Biol

In order for a tree to function efficiently, not only must its structure be sound but it must be living in balance with its surrounding climate and soil. Any alteration of this balance, eg by removal of branches, by feeding the soil or by altering the immediate surroundings of the tree, will have an overall effect on the tree's growth. It is, therefore, important that a tree surgeon should have an understanding of the structure and function of the various parts of the tree.

The tree basically consists of leaves, trunk and branches, root system and flowers.

Leaves

The leaves are the primary energy-manufacturing region of the tree, without which the plant could not produce growth.

Photosynthesis

By the process of photosynthesis the leaves are able to convert light energy into stored energy as carbohydrates inside the plant. In order to do this the raw materials of water, originally obtained via the root system in the soil, and carbon dioxide, from the surrounding air, are necessary. This reaction produces oxygen as a waste product which is returned to the air. For this reaction to take place light energy must be absorbed by the pigments present in the leaf, the most usual one being chlorophyll, a green pigment.

The overall reaction of photosynthesis can be summarised by the following chemical equation:

$$6CO_2 + 6H_2O \xrightarrow[\text{pigment}]{\text{light}} C_6H_{12}O_6 + 6O_2$$

Carbon dioxide	Water		Carbo-hydrate	Oxygen

The leaf structure is designed so that photosynthesis can be carried out efficiently. The leaves provide a large surface area so that the maximum amount of light can be absorbed. The pigments inside the leaf are concentrated in the tightly packed cells (palisade mesophyll cells) near the upper surface of the leaf so that they are in the position most able to receive light. The lower layers of the leaf are made up of very loosely packed cells (spongy mesophyll cells) linked to numerous pores or stomata in the lower surface of the leaf. This allows the quick diffusion of carbon dioxide into the leaf and the fast removal of waste oxygen from the leaf. The whole leaf is served by a vein system which transports water in the xylem cells to the palisade mesophyll and removes carbohydrates via the phloem cells from the leaf to the rest of the plant (fig 1a).

Although chlorophyll is the most common pigment in green leaves, other pigments may also be present, eg carotenes (orange), xanthophyll (yellow) and anthocyanin (red). These also assist in absorbing light. In a few species chlorophyll is not the main absorbing pigment and consequently the leaves do not appear green, eg in copper beech where anthocyanins are the main pigments in the outer leaves of the tree. In autumn when the light intensity is reduced the chlorophyll in many plants is not renewed and therefore other pigments present in the leaf are able to show through. This is one main factor which contributes to some species developing autumn colour.

Respiration

Once carbohydrates are produced by the leaf they are circulated in solution in the phloem cells to all parts of the plant. It is essential for all living cells in the plant to be supplied with carbohydrates which they can then convert into usable energy by the process of respiration.

To provide sufficient energy for growth the tree requires oxygen for aerobic respiration. The overall reaction is summarised by the following chemical equation:

$$C_6H_{12}O_6 + 6O_2 \xrightarrow{\text{enzymes}} 6CO_2 + 6H_2O + ENERGY$$

Carbo-hydrate	oxygen		carbon dioxide	water
			waste products	

Any carbohydrate which is not immediately required for respiration is stored inside the plant, mainly in the root system.

Since photosynthesis occurs only during daylight and when leaves are present on the tree it must therefore be an efficient process to produce sufficient carbohydrate to sustain respiration which occurs throughout the year in all the plant's living cells.

Transpiration

The second main function of the leaves is transpir-

Fig 1   Internal structure of leaf
a   Transverse section of leaf
b   Detail of stomata

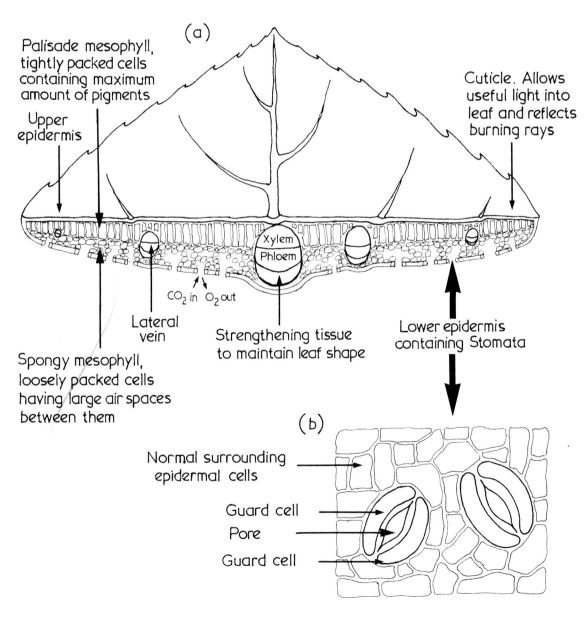

(a)

Palisade mesophyll, tightly packed cells containing maximum amount of pigments

Upper epidermis

Cuticle. Allows useful light into leaf and reflects burning rays

Xylem
Phloem

CO_2 in O_2 out

Lateral vein

Strengthening tissue to maintain leaf shape

Lower epidermis containing Stomata

Spongy mesophyll, loosely packed cells having large air spaces between them

(b)

Normal surrounding epidermal cells

Guard cell

Pore

Guard cell

ation. This is the loss of water by evaporation from the surface of the plant. Water will be lost from all exposed surfaces of the plant, and since the surface area of the leaves contributes a very large proportion of the overall surface area a great amount of water is lost via the leaves.

More important than this general water loss from the plant is the controlled transpiration occurring from the stomata mainly found in the leaf lower epidermis (fig 1b). Water is lost from stomata when the pores are open during the day, and the loss virtually ceases when the pores are closed at night. Since the opening and closing of stomata is controlled, the stomatal transpiration is also controlled to some extent.

Stomatal opening is controlled by the two guard cells surrounding the pore (fig 1b). When these cells are turgid they maintain their curved shape and the pore opens. Usually this will be during the daytime if a good supply of water is present. At night the guard cells become flaccid and lose their kidney shape and the pore therefore collapses. Stomatal transpiration of most trees accounts for about 90 per cent of the total water lost by the plant.

Vast quantities of water are lost by trees on warm, sunny days and sometimes the tree will have difficulty in replacing this water from the soil so that the plant wilts. The loss of water fulfils two important functions. Firstly, evaporation of water causes cooling which prevents the sun's rays burning the plant's organs. Secondly, the loss of water from the plant's leaves produces transpiration pull which provides a circulation system carrying water and nutrients up the xylem tissue in the tree from the roots.

Effects of external factors

The efficiency of the leaves can be affected by many factors. External environmental factors such as a reduction in light intensity, low temperatures, and a lack of water and nutrients in the soil will reduce the rate of photosynthesis and transpiration so that the leaves become inefficient. Some of these factors occur naturally in autumn, and in deciduous trees this results in leaf fall. In evergreen species, leaf fall occurs as the leaves age and again become inefficient.

Any reduction in the surface area of the leaf exposed to the light will result in the leaf becoming inefficient. Atmospheric pollution causing the leaf to be covered with dust and the stomata blocked with particles reduces photosynthesis and transpiration. Pests and diseases attacking the leaves are also important. Leaf feeders such as caterpillars, vine weevils and leaf miners greatly reduce the photosynthetic area of the leaf. Leaf suckers, eg

aphids, reduce the carbohydrate available to the plant as well as weakening the leaf structure. Leaf diseases may also have the same effect, for example leaf spot diseases, rusts and powdery mildew diseases reduce the green area of the leaf. Again the leaf will become inefficient, and pest and disease damage often results in premature defoliation of the tree.

Trunk and Branch System

Functions - support and conduction

The trunk and branches of a tree must fulfil two basic functions. The first is the general support of the plant to allow the leaves and flowers of the tree to develop in suitable positions to carry out their functions. It is essential for the tree to have a good support system so that it can achieve height dominance over other species and receive maximum light. Secondly the trunk and branches must provide a good transport system linking the roots and leaves. Therefore, large amounts of strengthening and conducting tissue must be present.

Strength is obtained in trees by the formation of wood which develops with age in the tree. The formation of wood (secondary thickening) occurs in both the stem and root areas of the plant in basically the same way. A ring of meristematic cambium tissue develops (fig 2a). This divides many times, producing each time an inner ring of cells which develop to form xylem tissue and an outer ring of cells which remain as cambium. Occasionally a third ring of cells is produced by the cambium dividing and this becomes phloem (fig 2b). The xylem cells develop into vertical tubes, and to provide them with strength and flexibility a hardened substance called lignin is developed as a spiral lining the tubes. After about five years the lignin becomes so thick that it totally blocks the tubes, producing dead cells which are wood. The lignin produces the characteristic dark colour of the heartwood of the tree compared with the lighter colour of the still living xylem cells forming the sapwood. The sapwood is responsible for the movement of water and nutrients up the tree. The phloem cells formed by secondary thickening carry carbohydrates down the tree and make up the bast wood (fig 2c).

The rate at which wood is produced depends on the plant species and on the surrounding environment. In the trunks and branches of most trees annual rings can be seen as the difference between the large, quickly produced, spring-formed xylem tubes and the previous summer and autumn production of smaller, closely packed xylem tubes (see fig 2d).

Most of the transporting system in the trunk

Fig 2   Internal structure of stem
a   Young stem
b   Initial wood development
c   Mature stem
d   Details section of mature stem

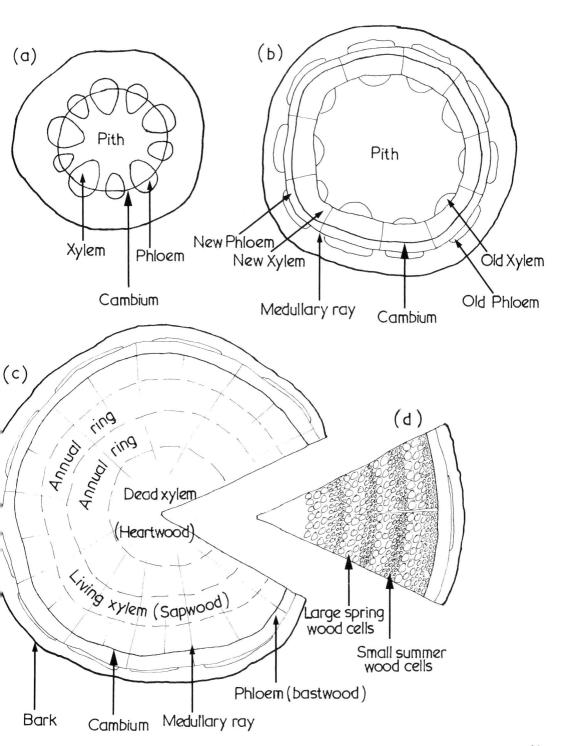

(a)

Pith

Xylem   Phloem

Cambium

(b)

Pith

New Phloem
New Xylem

Old Xylem

Medullary ray   Cambium

Old Phloem

(c)

Annual ring
Annual ring

Dead xylem

(Heartwood)

Living xylem (Sapwood)

(d)

Large spring
wood cells

Small summer
wood cells

Phloem (bastwood)

Bark   Cambium   Medullary ray

and branches is designed for conduction of materials up and down the tree. However, it is essential to have some movement of air and solutions across the tree and this is done via wood rays (medullary rays). These are lines of non-lignified cells positioned across the wood tissue. Since these cells are not strengthened these are the weak points in the trunk and branch system along which longitudinal cracks may develop, eg frost cracks.

At the same time as wood is being produced inside the tree, bark develops as a protective layer surrounding the living cells round the tree. This is produced by a ring of meristematic cork cambium tissue formed on the outside of the bast wood. The cork cambium divides to produce cork cells which build up on the outside of the stem. These cork cells gradually become blocked with an oily substance, suberin, and an antiseptic, tannin. These two substances enable the bark to protect the internal living tissues from environmental conditions and also help prevent the entry of harmful pests and diseases, eg elm bark beetle, wood borer, etc.

The bark itself is not a total barrier separating the interior of the tree from its environment. Gases for respiration and the waste products from respiration must be able to pass through. Consequently, there are areas of loosely packed cork cells in the bark called lenticels where gas exchange can take place. The lenticels can be seen on the bark and give some barks characteristic patterns when they are very obvious, eg cherry. The position of the lenticels often links with the internal medullary rays. They are the weak areas in the bark and are the usual points of entry by pests and diseases into otherwise healthy trees.

Effects of damage and healing capacity

The effects of damage to any part of the trunk or branch system of a tree will vary with the age and health of the plant. For any wound healing to occur, the meristematic cambium tissues are important. The natural response of the plant to wounding is a rapid division of the cambium tissue to form a callus over the surface of the wound. As healing continues the cork cambium tissue develops to form cork cells which become suberised and function in the same way as bark.

Surface wounds damaging only the bark tissue will normally callus over fairly easily. Deeper wounds which damage the conductive and protective tissue of the plant leaving the heartwood exposed may develop to form cavities. As the callus forms it can produce a cup-shaped lip which holds moisture causing the area round the cavity to rot away. The cavity then enlarges and can

remain moist owing to seepage of sap from the surrounding living sapwood, causing further breakdown of the wood. If a number of small cavities are in the same area the diseased wood will quickly join and the inner core of heartwood of the branch or trunk will decompose to leave a hollow shell. The junctions of large branches next to the area of decay are weakened. Eventually these may be lost, leaving only the hollow trunk standing.

Root System

Functions

Although a tree's root system is not usually obvious, it often extends over a much larger area than the canopy. The root system has three functions. Firstly, it must be strong to give anchorage to the plant. Secondly, it is responsible for the uptake of water and nutrients from the soil. Thirdly, it stores excess carbohydrate produced by photosynthesis.

Some trees possess a deep tap root which is usually longer and always thicker than the rest of the root system. This acts as the main anchorage root and it may also have the advantage of obtaining capillary water from the soil water table. The extra girth of this type of root also accounts for much of the plant's excess carbohydrate store.

Nearer the surface of the soil the tree will also have an extensive system of fibrous roots. These are responsible for the main uptake of water and nutrients from the soil. It is essential for the tree to have a good fibrous system in the top soil since this is the area where high soil-organism populations are decomposing organic matter and, therefore, where most nutrients are available. It is also the area where most use can be made of water percolating through the soil from rain.

The tips of the roots are most important for uptake from the soil. Since the tip of the root is the growing point, the young, unlignified cells are situated here; in addition, the epidermal cells of the root tip are modified to form root hairs. These root hairs are elongated epidermal cells which provide a large surface area of cell wall in contact with the soil for both nutrient and water uptake.

Water is taken into the root by the process of osmosis. For this to occur there must be a supply of capillary water forming a dilute soil solution surrounding the root hairs. This water will then be drawn into the concentrated cell sap of the root hair through the cell wall. Osmosis occurs across the root itself and water is eventually pulled into the xylem tubes and up the plant, mainly by transpiration pull.

Nutrients also are taken into the plant mainly

via the root hairs. For healthy growth all plants require certain essential nutrients. These are divided into those required by the plant in large quantities, ie nitrogen, phosphorus, potassium, calcium, magnesium and sulphur, and those equally essential but required in smaller amounts, ie iron, boron, zinc, copper, manganese and molybdenum. The tree must be able to obtain balanced quantities of all these nutrients. If any are lacking, the tree will show deficiency symptoms. Excess of a nutrient can be equally harmful.

The roots obtain nutrients in the form of ions in the soil solution. If a nutrient is in a larger concentration in the soil than inside the plant it will flow into the plant root down the concentration gradient. It is unlikely that all nutrients required by the plant will be present in sufficient amounts for this type of uptake to take place, and consequently it is possible for the plant to use energy to draw in required nutrients which are in lower concentrations in the soil. Once inside the plant, nutrients are circulated in solution in the transpiration stream.

Effects of adverse conditions

If the soil solution surrounding the roots has a very high nutrient content – this could be produced, for example, by excessive feeding of the soil – exosmosis will occur and water will be drawn out of the plant root hairs. This causes a breakdown of the root hair cell structure and permanent damage results.

Although the soil must contain sufficient water to produce a dilute solution round the roots, it is also essential for air to be available in the soil. In waterlogged conditions where no air is available the root cells cannot respire by aerobic respiration as previously described and have to respire anaerobically. This can be only a temporary form of respiration because the process is inefficient and not enough energy is produced to maintain normal plant growth. In addition, ethyl alcohol is formed as a waste product and this is toxic to the plant. Trees which are not adapted to waterlogging will show shallow, stunted root systems because the growth points of the roots have been killed by the alcohol.

Other conditions apart from waterlogging may cause oxygen to be unavailable to the root. For example, compaction of the soil by machinery, roadways, or piling up of soil on the surface prevents oxygen from entering the soil as well as causing physical damage to the root by pressure.

The plant relies totally on the root system to replace water lost by transpiration. If the rate of transpiration exceeds the rate of water uptake, the plant will show signs of wilting and will eventually die. This may be due to drought conditions in the soil or to a poor root system. Hence, in a situation where the root system may not be efficient, eg in a newly transplanted tree, an anti-transpirant is used as a temporary measure to prevent excess water loss. This must be only a temporary situation because it will reduce the circulation system of nutrients up the plant.

Any damage occurring to a tree's root system will directly and proportionally affect the growth of the tree. Root pruning as a deliberate method of controlling tree growth was a common practice in the past. The same effect will occur if damage is caused to the tree root system by pests and diseases, eg cockchafer damage to young trees, *Phytophthera* damage to young roots.

Flowers

Flowers are essential for the sexual reproduction of trees. Pollen is produced in the male part of the flower, ie the anther, and ovules are developed in the female ovary. After pollination and fertilisation occur the ovule develops to form the seed which may be protected by a fruit formed from the ovary. If pollen is transferred from one plant to another in pollination, the seed eventually produced may contain a mixture of the best genetic information from both parent plants, so producing a young tree which is better than either parent.

From this chapter it can be seen that the tree is a complex system and that damage to or alteration of any part of the system will affect the overall functioning of the plant. If the tree surgeon's role is to change the plant system, he must do so without substantially reducing the efficiency of the tree.

2 Tree Surgery and the Law

D. Patch, BSc (For), ND Arb, MI For

Common Law

Ownership of trees

Over the years decisions made by the courts have established that a tree is an integral part of the land on which it is growing. As such it is possible to sell a tree as an item separate from the land only when the tree is to be cut for its timber. The owner of the land on which the tree is growing is, therefore, accepted as being responsible for the safety and maintenance of the tree. One exception to this rule exists, and that is the case of a tenancy. The responsibility for any trees on the land may be clearly defined in the tenancy agreement, but if this definition does not exist the legal position is very intricate and the advice of a lawyer should be sought. Cases have arisen where both the tenant and the landlord were considered responsible following damage caused by a tree growing on tenanted land.

The courts have accepted that although an owner has the right to the air above and the ground below his property it is not an offence for a tree to overhang the boundary and encroach on the neighbouring property. However, if the tree causes actual damage the courts have given consideration to whether or not the owner has been negligent. The courts suggest in fact that the owner of land supporting trees should have a knowledge about trees greater than a layman might be expected to exhibit. Furthermore, it has been suggested that the owner should inspect his trees *regularly*, calling in expert advice if he sees something untoward. This poses the question, what is regular? Ideally, trees should be inspected twice per year – once in the summer to see that the foliage is healthy and normal for the species, and again in the dormant season to check the structure of the tree for weaknesses and evidence of the presence of diseases.

In view of these court decisions it is important that a tree surgeon or arboriculturist giving advice should explain to the owner all the alternatives and put them into perspective. A final decision may then be made by the owner of the tree. Failure to observe this code may lead to the owner of the tree bringing an action against the adviser for damages, especially after the tree has caused damage to adjoining property.

Trees overhanging boundaries

If a tree overhangs the boundary and encroaches on the adjoining property the owner of the tree is not *ipso facto* responsible for the removal of the overhanging portion of the tree. He does not become liable until actual damage has been caused by the tree. What, therefore, may a neighbour do about the overhanging branches which he considers an embarrassment? He would be perfectly within his rights to remove the offending branches without prior permission from the owner of the tree. However, it is important that neither he nor his equipment cross the boundary during the operation. Care must also be taken to ensure that in cutting the branches he does not take more than his 'pound of flesh': that is, he must not cut beyond the boundary line even in an attempt to prevent the branches growing over the boundary. Having removed the branches and abated the nuisance, he must remember that the material cut from the tree is not his and as such he may not burn or sell the branches or fruit. If he unthinkingly disposes of the material he would be liable in law for 'conversion'. The owner of the tree is allowed to enter his neighbour's property and collect the material cut from the tree. When on his neighbour's property the owner of the tree should take care not to cause damage or be disorderly.

A contractor should make sure that the owner of the tree has given permission, preferably in writing, for the prunings to be disposed of before burning the material. Similarly, the contractor would be liable for 'conversion' if without permission from the owner of the tree he cut up the prunings and took them home for his fire. An overhanging branch may bear fruit but the contractor must resist the temptation to pick the fruit and eat it. Failure to resist this temptation would also leave him liable to a charge of 'conversion'.

As with the overhanging branches, it is not an offence to allow roots to encroach on to the adjoining property. In fact, no action would hold until actual damage caused by the roots had been proven. Generally attempts to prove damage caused by roots have met with something less than complete success. However, the owner of the land being encroached upon may remove the nuisance under the same conditions as prevail for the branches. The only aspect to bear in mind is that although there is a legal right to the air above and the soil below a property the neighbours are entitled to lateral support for their land. This should be considered if root pruning is undertaken. Where tree roots are considered to be a problem a neighbour may resort to chemicals to kill the roots. This technique would be acceptable provided there was no lateral percolation or seepage of the chemical on to another person's property (see Dangerous objects, below).

Trees on boundaries

As large properties and agricultural land become developed with modern high-density housing, more and more mature forest-type trees are being retained on the boundary between two dwellings. In such an instance a tree surgeon may be asked to say where the responsibility for the tree lies. It is, in fact, often difficult to define ownership and recourse may have to be made to the deeds of the properties. Unfortunately, such documents often include plans which are inaccurate or inexplicit and as a result they may be taken only as guidelines. In the event of a dispute between neighbours it may be necessary in the final instance to consult a qualified surveyor.

Where it is finally decided that the tree is astride the boundary one must assume that both neighbours would have the right to remove branches and roots which encroach on to their land. This could lead to a very interesting situation especially when considered in the light of the possible destruction of the stability of the tree. Generally, such cases are resolved amicably and the ownership of the tree is shared which includes the cost of work and any income from timber salvaged from the tree.

Dangerous objects

The law requires that the owner or occupier of property keeps under control any dangerous objects on the property. This category is usually accepted as being a mad dog, stock or water, but it can also include fires, poisonous trees and chemicals.

In the case of fire there are two hazards – the fire itself and the smoke from the fire. In the first instance where a fire becomes out of control and causes damage to adjoining property the owner of the fire will be expected to compensate for the damage. With regard to the smoke from the fire, it is not an offence to create smoke provided the fire is not a regular occurrence, or in a clean air zone. If the smoke becomes persistent or is produced too frequently a neighbour would have a just complaint in court of a nuisance being caused (see also under Statute Law, below).

There is no reason in law why a landowner should not grow poisonous plants on his land. The landowner would become liable for damages if the poisonous plants overhung the boundary and resulted in actual damage to his neighbour. This damage could be the death of a cow or horse which had eaten the foliage. Similarly, a person working on a poisonous tree allowing leaves and branches to blow over the boundary into the adjoining property would be liable for any resulting damage caused to that property. If, however, it could be proved that the poisonous material had been completely within the bounds of the owner's property – in other words, that stock had to cross the boundary to reach the material – the owner of the material would not be liable. This is because it is the responsibility of the owner of stock to fence that stock on to his own land.

A tree surgeon must also be very careful when using chemicals of any type because drift or percolation through the soil of insecticide, fungicide, anti-transpirants or any other chemical used in tree maintenance could result in damage to the adjoining property. It would be prudent, therefore, to apply chemicals on calm days only or find alternative treatments if a chemical is likely to find its way on to adjoining property (see also under Statute Law, below).

Statute Law

Tree preservation orders

Under the Town & Country Planning Acts, the Government is empowered to make orders to protect trees from mutilation and unnecessary felling. These powers have been generally delegated to the local planning authorities although the Government remains the ultimate arbiter.

The Town & Country Planning Acts state that a tree preservation order may be made in respect of trees of high amenity value. This has on occasions been accepted as including trees of historic interest. However, amenity and historic values are very subjective and a tree surgeon would be well advised to assume, in the first instance, that all trees may be the subjects of orders.

When first considering the work to be undertaken on any tree the tree surgeon should ascertain from the owner of the property and, if necessary, from the local planning authority whether or not an order is operative. Failure to investigate this matter fully or failure to include a disclaimer in correspondence would result in the tree surgeon being held equally responsible with the owner for breach of the order and the possibility of a fine not exceeding £400 or twice the value of the tree whichever is the greater. Where the offence is other than the lopping, topping or wilful destruction of the tree, the fine is £200. If it can be proved that the owner of the land on which the tree stands has, or is likely to gain, financial benefit from the destruction of the tree the offence becomes indictable and a higher court may impose an unlimited penalty and possibly even a prison sentence.

The situation is made even more complex and full of pitfalls for the tree surgeon by the introduction of the Town & Country Amenities Act, 1974. Under the terms of this Act similar penalties may be imposed by the courts for the destruction of trees which are not the subject of tree preservation orders but which are growing in designated conservation areas. Before work is undertaken on trees growing in a conservation area it is necessary to give six weeks' notice of the intended work. After this period, if no directive has been received from the local planning authority the work may be undertaken. Failure to give this notice will be considered an offence under the Act and the penalties will be as specified above. A tree surgeon would be well advised to check that he is fully familiar with the conservation areas in his district.

Where a tree preservation order is in force, it is generally necessary to apply to the local planning authority for permission to undertake work on the trees. However, the order states that no such permission is needed for the abating of a nuisance or the lopping or topping of trees which are dead, dying or have become dangerous. It must be assumed that these criteria may also be applied to the removal of dead wood and dangerous branches. Unfortunately, there is only one of these three categories which may be considered as relatively clear-cut and that is the dead tree; all trees are dying and potentially dangerous. It is, therefore, advisable for a tree surgeon to contact the local planning authority in all cases until a working understanding has been developed. Once the local planning authority knows the standard of work and integrity of a particular contractor, it will usually suffice for the tree surgeon to explain by telephone the work to be undertaken. This could then mean that the local planning authority would allow the contractor to undertake such work as bracing and cavity work without the delays involved in formal applications.

Where a protected tree, other than a tree growing in a woodland, is removed because it is dead, dying or dangerous or where the permission of the local planning authority is not required, the tree surgeon should be aware of the requirements first introduced in the Civic Amenities Act, 1967. That Act requires that a replacement tree must be established; the species and size of tree to be planted have to be agreed with the local planning authority. The replacement tree then becomes the subject of the tree preservation order just as the original tree had been. The only way round this requirement of the Act is to apply to the local planning authority for permission not to replant, ie to waive the replanting requirement. In order for the local planning authorities to police this replacement requirement, subsequent legislation (Town & Country Planning (Tree Preservation Order) Regulations, 1969) places a responsibility upon the owner of a tree to advise the local planning authority at least five days in advance of the felling. However, if the tree is immediately dangerous the work of felling may be carried out but the local planning authority should be advised immediately after the work has been completed.

Felling licences

A tree surgeon may on occasion be asked to undertake site clearance work or the felling of a number of trees for one owner. Before commencing work it would be as well for the contractor to ascertain what volume of timber is to be cut and if necessary advise the owner to apply to the Forestry Commission for a felling licence.

Licences are required under the terms of the Forestry Acts where an owner is cutting more than 825 cu ft (30m³, or about 8–12 mature trees) in one period of three months. A licence is also required if the amount of timber sold by the owner in the three-month period exceeds 150 cu ft (5m³ or about two mature trees). In this context one may assume that where a contractor gives the service of cutting down trees and takes the timber in recognition of the service the owner has 'sold' the timber.

Failure of an owner to obtain a felling licence may involve him in a fine not exceeding £10 or twice the value of the trees whichever is the greater.

Highways and trees

From time to time the Government has reminded the authorities responsible for the maintenance of highways of their responsibility to ensure that the highways are safe places for the public. As such the tree surgeon may become involved with the maintenance of trees growing within the curtilage of the highway. Further, and more controversially, the tree surgeon may be asked to advise on and meet the requirements of an order issued by a highway authority to prune or fell trees within private land at the request of the owner or of the highway authority. The particular cases in which an order to attend to trees may be made are: (i) to provide clear vision for motorists; (ii) to allow sun and wind to the road; and (iii) to ensure the safety of the highway users. Furthermore, the tree surgeon should be aware of the need for any new plantings of trees to be sited at least 15ft (5m) from the centre of the made-up carriageway.

The Highway Acts also state that it is an offence to light a fire within 50ft (15m) of the centre of a made-up carriageway. Anyone convicted of lighting a fire close to a road is liable to a fine not exceeding £2. However, in this connection the tree surgeon should notice that in Common Law a fire is regarded as a dangerous object and, as such, damage caused by the fire leaves the 'owner' of the fire open to claims for compensation. The damage caused by a fire may be the result of the fire burning out of control or of the smoke blocking visibility resulting in an accident on the adjacent highway.

When working with trees near to a road a tree surgeon must take every precaution to prevent the blockage of the road and to avoid any danger to the public. Similarly, he should make every effort to avoid having ropes or wires across the road without the appropriate notices and, if necessary, police co-operation.

Plant health

Britain is in a unique position in so far as the surrounding seas restrict the natural spread of pests and disease-causing agencies. In addition, Britain has a very equable climate which allows the growth of many exotic plants for both amenity and commerce. Some of these exotics form a link in the life cycle of pests and diseases which could affect the economic plants of the country. The Government has, therefore, introduced the Plant Health Act, 1967, in an attempt to prevent the introduction of organisms not already present in Britain. The Act also attempts to restrict the spread of the most damaging examples already in this country.

Under this Act imports of infected plants may be confiscated and destroyed without recompense. Also the Government may from time to time make orders directing the destruction of infected material, restricting the movement of infected material and prohibiting the preservation of live specimens. As these orders may be made under the Act or withdrawn without parliamentary debate a tree surgeon should maintain a vigilant watch on the mass media and if necessary consult the local representative of the Ministry of Agriculture, Fisheries and Food or of the Forestry Commission for up-to-date information.

The employer's responsibilities

All employers have a responsibility to provide safety equipment for an employee and to give instructional training in the use of the equipment. The employer will not be liable if, at the time of an accident, his employees fail to use safety equipment provided and deviate from the technique of working specified by the employer. Also if chemicals are used the correct protective clothing should be provided for, and worn by, the employees.

The law requires that an employer should insure his vehicles for damage or injury to third parties. This need for insurance extends to the need for the employer to have cover in respect of his employees so that if injury occurs to them the employer has no anxiety about meeting compensation claims. It is also advisable for the employer to carry public liability insurance in respect of damage caused to property or person by employees during the work of tree surgery.

Conclusion

These comments endeavour to summarise the details of court cases and digest the contents of parliamentary Acts. Some over-simplification has been inevitable and it may be necessary to refer to the Acts themselves or to consult a solicitor.

To sum up, it would be true to say that many of the problems associated with trees and tree work appear to be due to negligence. Where damage occurs to property as the result of a tree falling or a limb being fractured, the court decisions have tended to turn on whether the owner had been negligent. Similarly, a contractor who is negligent about fires, poisonous material, protecting the public and training his employees is also frowned upon by the law. Finally, the employee who fails to use correctly the safety equipment provided by the employer is negligent and is unlikely to receive full compensation for injuries. It is essential that everybody involved with trees should be fully attentive and cautious on all occasions.

3 Safety

Tree surgery is recognised as potentially the most dangerous aspect of arboriculture. The elements of height and fall as well as the handling of motorised cutting tools and heavy weights do give rise to many situations where accidents happen if staff are not properly trained, equipped and supervised. A considerable amount of blame is put on the accident-prone person. He is only someone who cannot, or does not, think ahead and cannot foresee what will happen as a result of his actions. Such people should swiftly be eliminated from the team and employed in a less dangerous capacity for their own safety and that of their fellow workers, and for the protection of the public and property.

Not all the dangers are associated with working at height. Many groundwork operations, eg felling, handling chain saws and chemicals, can be more destructive than the climbing accidents.

Those responsible for employing tree-surgery staff should ensure that all staff are acquainted with some basic safety rules or regulations. The following points illustrate the more general safety precautions that should be observed by all staff. More specific safety issues are covered later in this book when dealing, for example, with chain saws, actual work operations, use of ladders, etc.

There are four main aspects of safety: (i) safety of operators; (ii) public safety; (iii) care of property and surrounding features; (iv) implementation of safety regulations.

Safety of Operators

Health of staff

Medical examinations

One of the most basic requirements of tree-surgery staff is that they are physically and mentally fit.

Obvious disabilities will eliminate many, but some conditions, eg high blood pressure, heart conditions and even epilepsy, are not necessarily known even to the applicant. It is, therefore, sensible that all staff who are expected to work at heights should receive a medical examination. This should include eyesight and hearing, which take on special significance when communications between climber and assistant are of vital importance. Vertigo, on the other hand, will not be diagnosed until after the person has experienced working at height. Those pronounced healthy can develop illnesses which may impair judgement. Even a heavy head cold could make a person less efficient and potentially dangerous. If such persons are fit for work, perhaps some harmless ground work would be preferred to climbing.

Alcohol and drugs

The consumption of alcohol and non-prescribed drugs must be serious offences and strict penalties must be enforced. Staff on prescribed drugs will have this considered at their medical examination and the effects will be known.

First aid

However well-trained and safety-conscious staff are, accidents will occur. What is then important is that staff present can assist the injured by rendering the appropriate first-aid treatment. Many authorities and companies have first-aid courses for the staff and encourage attendance. With small mobile teams, it is recommended that all staff receive basic first-aid instruction. It is no use only one per team receiving training, as it may be he who is injured. Suitable courses can be provided by the local ambulance service or by the St John or Red Cross Ambulance Brigades.

The course should include preventing bleeding, treatment of suspected broken bones, whether or not to move the injured person, treatment of shock, and artificial respiration. Serious injuries are rare and minor troubles such as cuts or particles in eyes should not be neglected – they could lead to more serious disorders.

First-aid boxes should be carried in each mobile unit and at each depot. The foreman should be responsible for checking and replacing stock. The ambulance service should advise on stocking, but it should include an eyebath and ready diluted eyewash.

Accident procedures

There should be some agreed form of accident recording. Each mobile unit and depot should have an accident recording book and perhaps the foreman should be responsible for its completion. The record should include time of day, weather conditions, place, people involved and a brief but accurate account of how the accident occurred. These facts may become important if the injury results in prolonged absence from work or even permanent inability to work. Compensation claims will require factual statements, and the memory becomes blurred with time.

The foreman of any team should always ascertain the whereabouts of a telephone or professional medical help in case they are needed.

Training of staff

One of the characteristics of those who are good at tree work is often an extrovert personality, one that does not like to admit to not knowing every contingency likely to occur. This is potentially very dangerous. One of the essential features of every training scheme is to ensure that staff are fully aware of the dangers and safety elements of their work. However good or long a course may be, it will never cover every situation, and staff, unless under supervised instruction, must never attempt operations that they are not familiar with. New tools or techniques should be tried in accordance with strict safety procedures. Staff must always anticipate the results of any action they take. Much of the work is irreversible and it is not possible to learn by mistakes when working at height – there may not be a second chance.

Young, inexperienced staff should not be put into situations which they cannot handle. Even groundwork requires a number of skills, and supervision of traffic or of the public requires a person with authority and judgement.

Tree work teams

Much of tree surgery is teamwork. Staff should never work alone even on ground work. Help must always be within calling distance. Whenever two or more men are working together, one should be given command and the right to make final decisions. If for any reason this appointed person is absent or incapacitated, he should delegate his responsibilities.

In principle, only one man should work in a tree at any one time. If there are two, at some time their lifelines or tools could become tangled and this creates one more avoidable situation to concern the climber. However, some operations such as cable-bracing do require two climbers. Ground staff will always assist and advise on any dangers not apparent to the climbers.

Weather conditions

Unless in an emergency, staff should not carry out climbing operations in certain adverse weather conditions. Only the foreman on site can decide when it is potentially dangerous to climb or even when to call off the job and return to base. Weather forecasting by any reliable method – tuning into the radio is recommended – becomes an important early morning duty. Conditions that can make climbing hazardous are:

RAIN This is probably the most serious condition, giving rise to slippery branches and very unpleasant working conditions.

WIND In exposed sites, wind can easily upset the balance of a climber and cut branches can be carried some distance before falling, perhaps in an inconvenient place.

EXTREME COLD In normal conditions, an active worker will keep his blood circulating and himself warm. If, however, the operator becomes cold to the extent that his movements are impaired, he should not continue climbing.

ICE Glazed ice on branches is particularly dangerous and climbing should not be attempted unless in an emergency.

FOG When fog is so thick as to restrict vision from ground level to the climber, it must be considered dangerous.

SNOW Unless associated with any of the earlier conditions, snow is not normally a problem.

The above conditions make climbing dangerous, but often alternative work can be found at ground level or back at the base. The use of hydraulic platforms will avoid many of the delays caused in the past by these adverse weather conditions. If climbing must be carried out during such conditions, because of an emergency situation, only very experienced staff should be permitted to climb and as much ground help as necessary should be provided.

Clothing for tree-surgery staff

Owing to the comparatively small number of men employed in tree-surgery work in this country, very few clothes have been specifically designed for this industry. However, a fair range is available from industrial clothing and from that designed for forestry work, particularly from Sweden.

Staff require both personal and protective clothing. These may be supplied by the employer or at least made available at reduced rates. If items are considered compulsory, it is suggested that they should be issued free and charged for only if they are carelessly damaged or mislaid.

Climbers

FOOTWEAR Proper footwear for grip and protection is probably the most important item of personal clothing. Boots with rubber or rubber-substitute treaded soles, strong, waterproof uppers, lightweight, comfortable and with built-in steel toe-caps are considered ideal. Some climbers prefer calf-length boots but the majority of industrial boots as described above are ankle-length. In dry weather conditions some operators wear plimsolls but these offer no protection from cutting tools and branches. On no account should leather or nailed boots or shoes be used by climbers.

TROUSERS Heavy denim jeans or corduroys have proved to be perfectly adequate for climbing staff and are cheap. They should not be too loose-fitting or so tight as to restrict movement.

BODY CLOTHING Very few professional climbers work without a shirt more than once! In warmer weather, tough working shirts made from denim or other hard-wearing materials are commonly used. Close-woven or knitted pullovers will keep out autumn and spring chills. In the winter, some warmer clothing may be necessary and light denim jackets or anoraks should prove adequate. Nylon outer clothing tends to generate too much heat for comfort. Outer clothes should not be loose-fitting or have large patch pockets which may be caught in branches or equipment. A bib and brace is not suitable for the same reason but a pair of overalls will give complete protection and can be worn over other clothes. Scarves and ties are, of course, potentially dangerous.

HEADWEAR It is not normally recommended that climbers need to wear a safety helmet, as little should fall from above. The Forestry Commission's seed-collector's helmet looks useful but restricts communications with ground staff. With short hair it is questionable whether any headgear is required at all. A cap or anything similar would easily fall or brush off. Climbers with long hair, however, do create additional hazards for themselves and some means of controlling the hair is necessary. Headbands or even balaclavas should suit most needs.

A number of items of protective clothing and equipment should be made available as and when required.

GLOVES Few climbers would wear gloves as an aid to climbing, but when handling tree sealants, some chemicals and particularly when handling chain saws, gloves should be available. Close-fitting balistic gloves are suitable for chain saws whilst waterproof types may be required in connection with chemicals.

GOGGLES, VISORS, ETC A foreign body in the eye is one of the most common minor accidents in modern tree work, particularly when using light-weight chain saws at height. A range of goggles and visors is produced for industrial purposes and, when selecting, attention should be given to shatterproof types well-ventilated to prevent misting.

EAR PROTECTION A number of protective devices is available but the main problem is to retain adequate communications with ground staff. The main types are: (i) defenders or covers, attached either to a head or neck band or direct to a safety helmet; (ii) ear plugs or valves, inserted into the ear with removable washable rubber covers (these are very efficient but care must be taken to prevent inserting unclean objects into the inner ear); (iii) cotton-wool plugs, which give some temporary protection, though the manufactured plugs may work out expensive if used frequently over long periods.

Ground staff

Ground staff need all the basic equipment as mentioned but, in addition, all staff assisting under a tree should wear safety helmets. This also applies to managerial staff who may be paying only a brief visit to the site.

A range of types is available but important points to look for are that the helmet has been tested to British Standards, has an adjustable headband and, if possible, is comfortable and ventilated. Some argue for the peakless type, but the peak gives protection to the face and acts as a sun-visor. Chinstraps should not be necessary if the headband is properly adjusted.

Ground staff using noisy and dusty brushwood and stump cutters should wear goggles and gloves. Continued use of large chain saws with no or inadequate anti-vibration devices can give rise to a disorder known commonly as 'white-finger disease'. Many modern saws have adequate anti-vibration systems and these should prevent any damage. If, however, staff are using older saws without such devices, the wearing of gloves and the proper use of the saw, ie taking the weight off the hands and holding the saw lightly, will reduce the vibration problem. Gloves should be dry and spares should be available. A blunt chain or incorrectly adjusted depth gauges will increase the problem. It is recommended to stop the saw frequently rather than to work at long sessions of cutting. (See Forestry Commission Information Sheet: *Chain-Saws and Vibration Syndrome*, November 1970.)

Ground staff using noisy machines, eg chain

2 GT safety harness, nylon life line and prussik knot

saws, are liable to ear damage. Ear protectors have been described, but undoubtedly the best solution is to reduce the decibel level of the machines. If stricter regulations were to be imposed, manufacturers would quickly fit more efficient silencers.

Safety equipment for climbers

Even with the advent of hydraulic platforms there is, and always will be, the need for competent climbers. Until comparatively recently, no specialised safety equipment was available. In the early 1960s, some of the larger safety-conscious tree-surgery companies got together to attempt to correct this. Discussions with the Forestry Commission, manufacturers, local authorities and training establishments have resulted in a fairly comprehensive range of safety equipment being made available. The following are the main items.

Safety harnesses

See BS1397: *Safety Belts and Harness*, and Forestry Commission Record No 39. The only harnesses specifically designed for tree climbing are those produced by Barrow/Hepburn Ltd.

The first type produced was the Pakawa 'Savall' Harness, Forestry Commission pattern. This is a full harness with shoulder straps and a large 'D' ring for attaching the rope in the middle of the chest, designed for Forestry Commission staff for cone collecting. Although this is still used by some, it is now thought to be inappropriate for tree-surgery work.

During the mid-sixties, a true tree-climber's harness was produced, based on an American model. This was simply a seat strap and waist band, with the rope attached to 'D' rings at the ends of each seat strap. It was called the Tree Climber Body Harness. This harness was light and efficient and gave the sense of security without looking over-dressed. It quickly became popular with professional tree surgeons not only because of increased safety, but because it gave greater mobility in the tree, two free hands for working and greater productivity.

In 1970 an attempt was made to improve the design even further. The result was the Grip Tite 76 Tree Climber's Harness (2). Improvements included a much simpler and more efficient buckle, waist band 'D' rings enabling it to be used as a pole belt as well as a harness, and separate lengths of webbing to keep the seat strap down under the buttocks. Not all these modifications are as successful as was hoped. The waist band 'D' rings do work very well with a clog karabiner to give a useful adjustable pole belt (3), but when using it as a harness the rings tend to dig into the hips or lower rib cage and cause discomfort. The new

straps fail to hold the seat strap down and are perhaps even worse than on the original model. Recently further discussions have been held with the industry, educationists and the manufacturers, and, hopefully, these problems will be corrected.

Once equipped and trained in the use of the harness, it should become obligatory for the climber to use it during all climbing operations. Even a fall from a low branch can result in a broken neck.

Life-lines

The safety harness is used in conjunction with a life-line. Most tree surgeons use a 12mm dia (1½in circ) 45m (150ft) long nylon rope as a life-line. This has a safe working load of 500kg (1100lb) and being nylon has the built-in elasticity so essential to a life-line. This rope will, in fact, extend 48 per cent before breaking.

Strops

Strops for securing the climber in a selected position can be made out of 12mm dia nylon rope or purchased ready-made with an eye splice at each end. These can easily be attached and released from the safety harness with karabiners and give extra security, essential whilst still training or when in a particularly awkward situation. Lengths can vary from 2m to 3m (6–10ft).

Pole belts

When there is no anchor point above or when topping out trees, a safety harness cannot be used. Therefore, pole belts are required. As already mentioned, the GT76 harness can be adapted to use as a pole belt using the normal life-line and a clog karabiner. Other pole belts are produced for the GPO and can be used safely in tree work.

All harnesses and pole belts should be made to BSI standards.

Harnesses and pole belts must be inspected, before use by the operator, for any defects. Points to look for are:

1 Stitching should be secure and not frayed.

2 The Barrow/Hepburn terylene harnesses have a red core, and if at any time this red core shows through, the harness must be destroyed.

3 Any cuts, burns or scratches could weaken the harness.

Clips and karabiners

The life-line has to be attached to the harness and, to work efficiently, there has to be some mechanism

3   Climbing irons and clog karabiner used as a pole belt

to control the rate of descent. Two methods are available:

1   The life-line is passed over the anchor point, back down to the harness and tied to the 'D' rings with a bowline, leaving a 1·3m length of rope free. A karabiner can be placed on to the 'D' rings first to save time when manoeuvring in the tree. The end length of rope is tied to the rope going down the tree (2). The knot used is known as a sliding hitch (fig 3, page 33) and is more commonly called a prussik knot as it is used as an alternative to the prussiker clip. The effect is that, when the knot is released, the weight of the climber jams the turns and locks the climber in position. By holding the knot and pulling down, the turns are released and the climber can descend at a controlled rate.

2   Use of the prussiker ascending clip, as used in mountaineering. This gives the same action as the knot and is much faster to fit and remove. Some professional tree surgeons prefer this device, but the main fault is that the rope can jump out and, if the climber is not prepared, there is nothing to stop him falling (4). Personally, I would never recommend using the clip, since the knot is fool-proof and requires only a fraction more time to tie.

There is perhaps the need for a better-designed clip. Other descending devices have been tried but none has yet answered the need.

The karabiners used for attaching the life-line to the harness and attaching tools and equipment to the clips on the harness are very efficient devices. A number of makes are available. The manual screwgate type is the main type used and it is essential to ensure that the gate is secure before climbing. The self-locking types are normally much heavier and larger and are used only on strops.

It is normal practice to issue each full-time member of a tree-surgery team with his own set of safety climbing equipment. He is then responsible for its proper use, maintenance and storage.

Climbing irons

The use of climbing irons should be restricted to trees that are to be felled; the scars that the irons make will then be of little consequence.

In practice, irons are perhaps used more frequently, particularly on very large trees above ladder height and with no climbing branches. If used only for the ascent and then removed before working, little damage will be done. They are, undoubtedly, a very useful climbing aid if climbers are trained in their use, and if correct irons are selected.

4   Unsafe practice of using a prussik ascending clip as a descending device

The important points to consider are:

1   Tight, secure, comfortable fitting. Better-quality irons have adjustable calf lengths and firm pads between the metal uprights and the leg.

2   The gaff or spike which supports the climber. The shape of this is critical. Many Post Office types have very short gaffs for use on telegraph posts and are not suited to rough-barked trees.

Although very expensive, the type incorporating all the above features is the Bashlin climbing iron which is imported from America (3).

Climbing bicycle

This piece of equipment (5), used by the Forestry Commission for cone collecting, has little practical use in tree surgery. Perhaps for occasional jobs on trees with very high, clear stems which ladders will not reach, or where irons are not allowed, the bike may have its use.

Tools, equipment and materials

Full details of tree-surgery tools, equipment and materials – including safety factors – are given in the following chapters. It is most important when considering safety to pay particular attention to correct selection, and to ensure that operators are fully conversant with their safe and proper use and that time is allowed for adequate maintenance.

Many modern tree-surgery tools are potentially very dangerous and in untrained or foolish hands are lethal weapons. There are literally dozens of morbid stories to be told of death and mutilation caused by the incorrect use of power tools, particularly chain saws and winches. Most tools have their dangers, and ladders are the cause of a disproportionate number of accidents. The proper use of chemicals is of vital importance, not only for the safety of the operator but also for the public and wildlife. All cutting tools should be covered when not in use and kept well clear of ropes and harnesses.

Without doubt, blunt tools are far more dangerous than those that are properly sharpened. A blunt axe will bounce off the wood rather than sink in and could fly anywhere. Likewise, a blunt or improperly sharpened chain saw will need to be forced through the wood. This will damage the saw and put the operator at far greater risk. Machines that will not start cause frustration and impatience, again increasing the chance of an accident.

Public Safety

Much tree surgery is carried out in public areas; in fact, it is difficult to justify tree surgery in any

other than public areas. It is, therefore, essential that due care is given to the public in proximity to the operations.

Traffic warning and control

Before work commences on roadside trees, the local police should be informed as they may prohibit work at certain peak traffic hours and will advise on traffic warning and control. It is unlikely that they will send assistance unless a traffic jam or some calamity occurs. The local highway authority may also be able to give advice on roadside operations.

The first important issue is to give the motorist adequate warning of any danger ahead. If the tree work means blocking the highway or pavement, approved warning signs should be displayed on both sides of the road giving ample braking distance. The Ministry of Transport Regulations, 1972 (Table 1), state the sizes, numbers and distances of road signs, dependent upon the average speed of traffic.

Table 1: Ministry of Transport Regulations, 1972: Road Signs

Average speed of private cars	Distance of first sign from road works	Size of signs (inches)	Number of signs required
Up to 30mph	Not less than 50yds	24	2
30–40	50–120	30	2 or 3
40–50	120–300	36	3 or 4
50–60	300–500	48	4
Over 60	500–800	60	4

Road signs must comply with Traffic Signs Regulations & General Directions, 1964, No 1857, Schedule 1, Parts i, ii and iv and The Ministry of Transport Regulations, 1972. The Ministry No 562 sign (a red triangle with a black exclamation mark on a white background) is the advanced warning sign of danger ahead. Beneath this may be displayed a number of captions with permitted variants. The captions suitable for tree surgery are either TREE CUTTING or FALLEN TREE, as shown on page 62. It is not illegal to use other signs but, if the above signs are not used, the operators will almost certainly be found liable if an accident occurs.

In addition to the signs, other equipment may be required. Red and white cones are very useful to divert traffic round an obstruction; they are light and durable and should have reflective paint. When blocking a major part of the carriageway, STOP/GO signs or even temporary traffic lights may be necessary. If leaving obstructions over-

5 Tree climbing bicycle and strop attached to GT harness

night, illuminated warning must be given. The amber flashers or conventional road danger lamps should suffice.

Pedestrian control and protection

Pedestrians, particularly children and busy mothers with prams, are a real problem. Tree work appears attractive to the young and a nuisance to the busy mum if you attempt to block her route. Very careful attention must be given to all pedestrians and this will require adequate tactful ground staff and good communication with the climber. It may be easier to stop the operation rather than the pedestrian. Pedestrian barriers are not the only answer, as these cannot be understood by the very young or be seen by the blind.

Site supervision

At no time should tools, particularly cutting tools, ropes and ladders, be left unattended. When staff do leave the site, no dangerous situations should be allowed to develop. Holes should be back-filled or warning barriers erected. Logs should be made secure so that they cannot roll and fires extinguished.

Fires

Fires are a great source of danger to all and in many areas fire lighting is prohibited. Where fires are permitted, they must not cause a nuisance either to road users or to local house occupiers (see Chapter 2).

Again, site supervision is of great importance, and children particularly must be kept well clear of the fire site. Fires must be completely extinguished before leaving the site, and this may mean that stoking should be finished by early afternoon, the ashes to be cooled by water or soil. One particular problem concerns fires on peat soils where the layers of peat could carry the fire underground. If fires are necessary a deep trench, down to the subsoil, should be dug around the fire site.

Staffing

All operations involving control of the public will need very careful planning and adequate ground staffing. Young, inexperienced staff should not be given the task of controlling traffic or the general public, where a person of authority and judgement is required.

Care of Property and Surrounding Hazards

Observation

It is the responsibility of management to note and allow for all surrounding features and problems when first planning an operation. However, some points may be missed, and the foreman, and indeed all staff, will need to keep a constant look-out for any obstacles or dangers.

The following surrounding features and hazards are ones that frequently cause problems.

Overhead power and telephone lines

Very careful attention should be given to see if any overhead lines are in proximity to the operation. Power lines are a particular problem to the operator and a number of men have been killed through negligence or lack of appreciation of the dangers involved. Medium and low voltage lines pass along many of our roads and through gardens to domestic dwellings. Electricity board staff attempt to keep the trees clear of lines but frequently trees need to be felled or pruned over or between lines. It is generally accepted that no tree-surgery staff should work on a tree where any part of that tree is within 3m (10ft) of a live line. If the tree is nearer, due warning should be given to the electricity board so that the power can be turned off or the line dismantled. Most boards will provide this service without charge if sufficient notice is given. Electricity board staff often work on trees less than 3m from lines, but they are trained in distinguishing low from medium voltage lines and live from earth lines, and are equipped with non-conductive tools and equipment.

Telephone lines do not present quite the same problems but, again, the GPO should be requested to dismantle lines that are in the way. A broken line will not only cause annoyance to the owner or client but could break the bracket and fixing to the house. The repair bill could well exceed the profit!

Underground services

Although not so obvious, underground services – such as water, gas, drainage, sewerage and electricity – can easily be fractured if heavy limbs or trunks are dropped over them or roots disturb them when winching out stumps. Again, supervisors should check for likely underground service routes by the presence of manhole covers and drains or from plans.

Surrounding structures and features

The proximity of structures and features to the tree will determine the method of operation. Trees may have to be felled in sections or have branches roped off to avoid damage. Time must be allowed for this in any bonus scheme timing. It may, on occasion, be possible and quicker to remove an object such as a fence or young tree or shrub rather than try to work round it. With agreement

from the owner or client, it may be cheaper to reinstate damaged grass areas rather than fell a large tree in small sections. Care must be taken to protect surrounding trees and, if using a tree as winch anchor, adequate protection should be given (see Anchoring Systems in Chapter 4 and illustration on page 42).

(see Anchoring Systems in Chapter 4 and illustration on page 42).

Implementation of Safety Regulations

If an employer plans to implement and maintain safety regulations, thought should be given to the following.

Organisation

All units need to be organised, supervised, staffed and equipped so that all the factors mentioned are practicable.

Regulation sheet

If a regulation sheet is to be produced, the foreman and experienced staff should be involved with its planning so that all rules are practical and clear penalties agreed. Once it has been formulated, all staff should be given a copy and copies should be displayed in their mess-room. All new staff should receive a copy during their induction training.

Unions

Agreement should be reached with the staff's union or spokesman to see that the rules do not affect the conditions of service or earning capacity.

Bonus schemes

If a bonus scheme is in operation, allowance must be made on the rate for the job to allow for all safety procedures.

Discipline

Any serious breach of regulations must be disciplined at once and with agreed penalties. Records should be kept of any disciplinary action.

Accidents

Any accidents should be fully discussed and the reasons made public.

General

All men must be safety-conscious at all times and managerial staff must set an example. It must be the responsibility of all staff to keep a vigilant watch for any dangers, and not just rely on the foreman. Encouragement should be given to staff to suggest improvements in techniques or safety factors.

4 Tools and Equipment

Tree surgery is still a comparatively minor industry and until recently very few tools or equipment were specifically designed for the work. This is changing; with the advent of tree-surgery sales services, more and more purpose-made equipment will be made available. Use can also be made of a great range of tools and equipment from other industries and sports, eg mountaineering ropes, ladders and hydraulic tools from general industry, and many hand and mechanical tools from the forestry industry.

As mentioned in previous chapters, the correct selection, use and maintenance of tools and equipment are essential safety factors for efficient and productive work.

Ropes

Ropes are essentially a safety factor and in order to have confidence in their use, operators should know of the types available, select the right rope for the job and be familiar with the correct use and maintenance of ropes. If any of these points are overlooked or ill-considered, the whole purpose of using a rope may be lost and the results can be disastrous.

Types and qualities of ropes

Ropes can be formed or laid in many ways. The three-strand or hawser lay, with a right-hand construction, is the type normally used in tree work.

The three main types of ropes used in tree surgery are man-made fibre ropes, natural fibre ropes and steel wire ropes. Steel wire ropes are discussed in detail in Chapter 8, under Cable Bracing.

Man-made fibre ropes

Artificially or synthetically produced fibres have revolutionised many industries. The advantages of synthetic fibre ropes are many, although there is still a use for natural fibre ropes in tree-surgery work.

Man-made fibre ropes, in general terms, are immune to damage from water, rot and fungal organisms and are unattractive to rats, mice and insects. Some do lose some of their tensile strength if exposed to sunlight. However, the amount of sunlight experienced in this country and the working situation, ie beneath or in the shade of trees, results in such a minute loss that it is of little significance.

Of the man-made fibre ropes, the following can be considered for tree work.

NYLON A polyamide derived from coal. Nylon is the strongest man-made fibre rope and its important quality is its high energy absorption capacity. It has an approximate 48 per cent ultimate extension. It has a comparatively high melting point of 250°C (482°F) and is resistant to attacks from alkalis, oils and organic solvents. See BS3977: *Polyamide (nylon) Filament Ropes*, and BS3104: *Nylon Mountaineering Ropes*.

TERYLENE A polyester derived from oil. Size for size, heavier than nylon rope and less strong. Has a 38 per cent extension, resists acids and is unaffected by bleaching agents, oils and organic solvents. See BS3758: *Polyester (terylene) Filament Ropes*.

POLYPROPYLENE Again derived from oil. Of the various types, only the fibrefilm is considered. Size for size, much stronger than natural fibre ropes and little more expensive. The lightest man-made fibre rope. Only a 28 per cent extension, but a low melting point of 165°C (329°F). Resistant to acids, alkalis and oils.

Natural fibre ropes

See BS2052: *Ropes made from coir, hemp, manila and sisal*. Natural fibre ropes, as the name implies, are constructed from fibres extracted from organic materials. In general, they are not resistant to rot, mildew and chemicals, and like other plant material will decompose if left in a damp condition. Despite these obvious disadvantages, compared with man-made fibre ropes, they do have a part to play in tree surgery because they do not stretch and are inexpensive. They do not melt but will begin to char at 150°C (302°F).

The two main types considered are:
MANILA The fibre is produced from the plant *Musa textilis*, grown in the Philippine Islands. It is marketed in various grades and is more expensive than sisal, but stronger.
SISAL Produced from the plant *Agave sisalana*, grown in East Africa. Two types are supplied: (i) Waterproofed – absorbs little water, therefore less prone to rot. It is easier to handle than the untreated type. (ii) Untreated or white sisal. Cheaper than waterproofed sisal and as strong.

Selection and use of ropes

Selection of ropes

Knowing the types available, a rope can be selected with the best qualities for the job to be done. The strengths of ropes are an important consideration (Table 2). Other considerations such as elasticity, maintenance and weight can make the selection for use fairly automatic.

Table 2: Breaking loads of ropes (manila 100%)

Type	Breaking load (%)
Manila Grade 1	100
Sisal and Manila Grade 2	88
Nylon	250
Terylene	200
Polypropylene Fibrefilm	167

NYLON   Ideally suited as a life-line because of its strength and stretch. It is unlikely that the heat generated by friction in tree work would melt a nylon rope. Used almost exclusively as a life-line.
TERYLENE Being heavier, weaker and with a lower extension, it has no significant advantage over nylon as a life-line, and would be very expensive for general-purpose branch work. Not commonly used in tree surgery.
POLYPROPYLENE FIBREFILM   Because of its very light weight and its greater strength in comparison with natural fibres, also its durability, looked to be an ideal rope for branch slinging; strength for strength, it is little more expensive than manila grade 1. However, owing to its low melting point of 165°C (329°F), it has been proved that in some tree-surgery work the friction generated resulted in breakage. It is, therefore, considered dangerous apart from, possibly, load-tying on trucks. It is used by electricity board tree-work teams because of its non-conductivity qualities.
MANILA The high cost and excessive stretch of nylon and terylene, and the melting of polypropylene make manila an attractive alternative for general-purpose branch work and load-carrying operations.
SISAL It has the same attractions as manila, but is less strong. It is frequently used as manila and for light tool lines.

Sizes of ropes

Ropes were formerly measured by the circumferences in inches, but with the change to metrication they will be known by millimetres diameter. The conversion is quite simple: multiply inches circumference by 8 to give millimetre diameter – eg 1in circumference rope × 8 = 8mm dia, 3in circumference rope × 8 = 24mm dia. A nylon life-line is normally 12mm dia (1½in circ), a light tool line would be 8mm dia (1in circ), and branch ropes would be 16mm dia (2in circ), 20mm dia (2½in circ), or 24mm dia (3in circ).

The lengths of the operational rope could vary with the normal size of tree being worked, but 40–45m (140–150ft) lengths are most commonly used. Ropes are marketed in coils. A coil was a nautical length of 120 fathoms or 240yds. In future they will be 220m. If ropes are purchased in coils, five working lengths can be cut per coil.

Safe working loads of ropes

It is normally accepted that the maximum load that should be put on to a rope, the safe working load, is no more than one-sixth of the breaking load. This reduction may at first appear excessive and exaggerated, but consider the following reasons.
INACCURACIES IN ESTIMATING WEIGHT OF BRANCHES It is almost impossible to calculate accurately the weights of branches or trunks of trees in the field without elaborate measuring and weight tables. Many arboricultural textbooks in the past have tabled weights of volumes of green wood. The actual weights of timber depend on species and water content, eg 1 cu ft of poplar with an 80 per cent water content will weigh approximately 37lb. A comparable piece of oak could weigh 60lb. Few operatives carry weight tables and calculators, so in practice fairly rough estimates are made and inaccuracies occur.
REDUCTION IN STRENGTH DUE TO APPLICATION OF KNOTS   Bridon Fibres & Plastics Ltd carried out tests on a number of types of ropes and measured the percentage of retained strength of knotted ropes. The following is part of the tests' results:

	Nylon	Sisal
Bowline	58%	63%
Timber hitch	55%	94%

It can be seen that the application of a knot can reduce the breaking strength by up to 50 per cent.
DETERIORATION WITH AGE   Breaking loads are calculated on new ropes; all ropes, particularly natural fibre, will deteriorate and be weakened with age.
MECHANICAL WEAR AND TEAR   Continued use and chafing over rough surfaces must weaken the rope.

It is impossible to measure the last two points, but they must be allowed for when arriving at a safe working load.

Table 3 shows types, sizes, breaking and safe working loads, and weight of ropes considered for use in tree surgery.

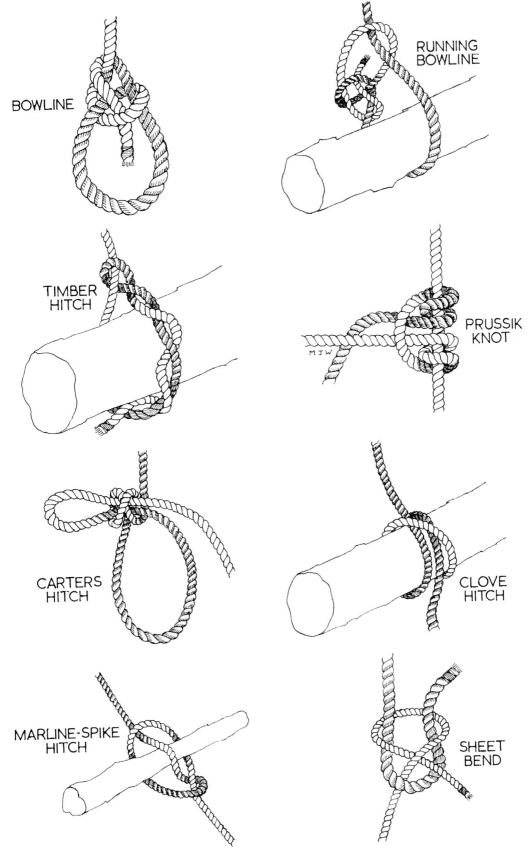

BOWLINE

RUNNING BOWLINE

TIMBER HITCH

PRUSSIK KNOT

MJW

CARTERS HITCH

CLOVE HITCH

MARLINE-SPIKE HITCH

SHEET BEND

Fig 3   Knots commonly used in tree surgery

Table 3: Sizes, loads and weights of ropes

Size		Breaking load		Safe working load		Weight	
Inches circ	mm dia	lb	kg	lb	kg	lb/ 100ft	kg/ 100m
NYLON							
1½	12	6,610	3,000	1,101	500	6.4	9.4
POLYPROPYLENE FIBREFILM							
2	16	7,840	3,500	1,306	586	7.8	11.5
3	24	15,700	7,600	2,616	1,266	17.5	26
MANILA GRADE 1							
1	8	1,190	540	198	90	3.7	5
1½	12	2,360	1,070	398	178	7.1	10
2	16	4,480	2,030	746	338	13.0	19
3	24	10,080	4,570	1,680	761	27.0	40
SISAL							
1	8	1,060	480	176	80	3.7	5
1½	12	2,100	950	350	158	7.1	10
2	16	3,920	1,780	653	296	13.0	19
3	24	8,960	4,060	1,493	676	27.0	40

Figures as quoted by Bridon Fibres & Plastics Ltd.

It is not feasible to expect operators to memorise and retain the safe working loads of all ropes used and, like weight tables, it is unlikely that SWL tables would be carried. What is important is that staff have an intelligent appreciation of ropes and branch weights and can select a rope of adequate strength and qualities to carry out the operation.

Knots used in tree-surgery operations

The correct use of knots is important for three reasons. First, an incorrect knot could seriously weaken the rope and reduce the breaking load. Second, an incorrect knot can slip or jam. Third, all the safety reasons for using ropes will be jeopardised if the knot fails to hold.

There is considerable variation of knots used for different operations in tree work, but the following are the most commonly employed (fig 3).

BOWLINE KNOT A very safe loop knot that should never collapse before the breaking load is reached. Used to secure the life-line to the safety harness.

RUNNING BOWLINE A variation of the bowline where a safe loop knot can be pulled up to lock on to a branch. Very useful where the desired anchor point cannot be reached.

PRUSSIK KNOT A sliding hitch which is used to control descent, in conjunction with a safety harness. When released will jam and prevent descent. Hand pressure will release and the operator can descend at a controlled rate.

FIGURE OF EIGHT KNOT This is a terminal knot tied in the end of a rope to prevent other knots coming undone. Used in tail end of rope after tying prussik knot.

CLOVE HITCH A general-utility jamming hitch to secure a rope to another object or to secure two objects together. Commonly used to fasten a ladder to a branch or to suspend flaked ropes in the stores area.

TIMBER HITCH A simple secure hitch which jams and holds by the weight of the object it is carrying. Used almost exclusively for securing a rope to a branch when being lowered. Particularly convenient as it falls apart when the load is off. It may often be necessary to tie a half-hitch before the knot. This will prevent the branch splitting and will help hold together dead or rotting branches.

CARTER'S HITCH This very useful hitch is used as a pulley or to tension a rope. Its applications are many but common examples in tree work are to create extra pull by the ground staff when pulling over a tree or pulling off a branch, and to tie down loads on lorries. Also known as waggoner's hitch.

MARLINE-SPIKE HITCH A little-known hitch tied with a short length of wood to obtain a more secure hold on a rope when pulling. Used in conjunction with a carter hitch.

SHEET-BEND A very useful simple bend for tying ropes together, particularly those of unequal thickness or texture. Used when pulling up heavy branch ropes or tying on equipment with a strop.

Securing ends of ropes

When ropes are cut, the ends must be made fast or secured to prevent fraying (fig 4). Common methods of securing the ends of ropes are:

WHIPPING WITH CORD There are two methods: simple or temporary whipping, and sail-maker's whip which gives a much stronger, more permanent hold. Nylon ropes can be whipped and the ends burnt to seal.

SPLICING This is a far more secure means of preventing a rope undoing. Again there are two main methods: back splicing, to leave a tapered heavy end in the rope; and eye splicing which will give a secure loop in the end of the rope.

Care and maintenance of ropes

General care of ropes

Always flake ropes when not in use. Make as large a flake as possible, consistent with storage space. Flake clockwise for right-hand laid ropes (6). Keep ropes dry if possible, particularly natural-fibre ropes. Keep all ropes clear of mud and loose sand or grit. Dirty ropes can be cleaned with water and dried naturally in a well-aired, frost-free store. Never walk on ropes. Avoid running ropes over or around sharp edges. Never pull out a kink formed in a rope but rather run it out by hand. Avoid tangling ropes; the ground staff should keep ropes clear of twigs and branches. Keep all ropes clear of cutting tools whilst at work, during transit and in

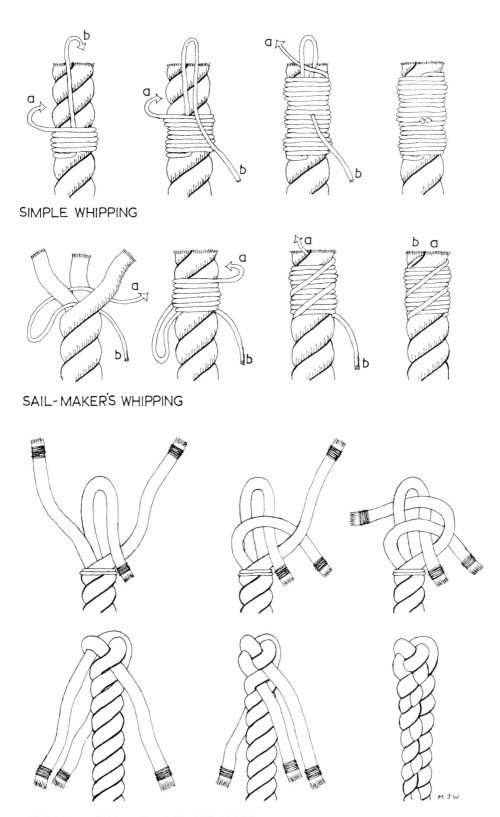

SIMPLE WHIPPING

SAIL-MAKER'S WHIPPING

CROWN KNOT AND BACK SPLICING

Fig 4   Securing ends of ropes

the store. Keep ropes clear of chemicals, oils, batteries, etc.

Inspection and maintenance of ropes

Before using a rope, it should be undone from its flake and run through the hands so that any signs of cuts, abrasions, burns or other indications of damage or wear will become apparent. More occasionally, perhaps monthly, a more detailed inspection should be carried out. The rope should be unlaid at intervals, and checked for internal signs of dusting or powdering. The ends of the ropes should be inspected to ensure that the whipping or splicing is intact.

Cleaning ropes can be a problem. Mud has already been mentioned, but more of a problem is tree paint – particularly the bitumastic types. Cleaning with chemicals can be carried out, and Table 4 indicates, as a general guide, the resistance of ropes to various chemicals.

Table 4: Resistance of ropes to chemicals

	Acids	Alkalis	Solvents
Natural Fibre	Poor	Poor	Good
Nylon	Poor	Good	Good
Polypropylene	Good	Good	Poor

Storage

Ropes should be stored in a frost-free, well-ventilated area. If wet they should not be force-dried, particularly natural fibre ropes. They are best suspended in their flakes from overhead bars (6). The common practice of storing life-lines in a canvas bag is satisfactory if the ropes are dry, but if wet they should be dried as mentioned.

Space should be allowed in the van or truck for the storage of ropes well clear of cutting tools.

If, on inspection, a rope is considered dangerous it should be destroyed. A dangerous rope left lying about could be re-used. Adequate spare ropes must be carried in stock.

Ladders

With the development, over the last few years, of safety harnesses and hydraulic platforms the role of the ladder in tree-surgery work has changed. Although large ladders (15–20m) are still used, the majority of operators use only a more portable ladder for access into the crown of the tree. Safety and portability are essential qualities and these should not conflict if care is given to right selection and proper use.

Types and qualities of ladders

The two main materials from which ladders are manufactured are aluminium and wood. Fibre-glass is used but mainly for smaller domestic types. Ladders are available in three main sizes: single section; push-up, double or triple; and rope-operated pull-up, double or triple.

Wooden ladders

See BS1129: *Specification for timber ladders, steps and trestles and lightweight stagings*.

Many of the old school of tree-surgery staff would never use any other ladders than those made from wood. They are solid, secure, warm to touch in winter and normally cheaper than alloy types. However, they are very heavy, particularly the large three-section types, and require regular maintenance. Only very good quality ladders should be purchased. This applies equally to both types, but wooden ladders, being made from natural materials, are far more variable.

The stiles (uprights) are normally made from pine, hemlock or spruce. They must be straight-grained and free from knots. The rungs, either round or oblong, should not protrude through the stiles, should be securely fixed and are usually made from ash or oak. Many will have tie rods at every fourth rung but quality manufacturers may say they are unnecessary. Steel cables along the stiles are of more value and prevent the ladder collapsing in the event of an accident and, if correctly tensioned, will bow the ladder to counter-act the weight of the climber.

Aluminium ladders

See BS2037: *Specification for aluminium ladders, steps and trestles*.

Most tree-surgery units are mobile with modern climbing aids; ladders when used are only to give access into the crown and are removed when the climber is secure in his safety harness. Therefore, most units will use aluminium ladders which have a main quality of lightness. They are also virtually maintenance-free. They are cold to handle and are much more expensive than their wooden counter-parts.

Selection of ladders

For mobile units a two or three section push-up aluminium ladder opening to 10–12m is considered ideal, being light, easy to handle and transport and maintenance-free.

If larger ladders are required, especially those with rope-operated pulleys, the wooden ladder has many advantages. The extra weight of the aluminium stiles for the pulleys will almost eliminate the weight advantage and their cost will be very high. Electricity board staff will use only wooden ladders as they are less conductive than aluminium.

6   Ropes flaked and suspended in store

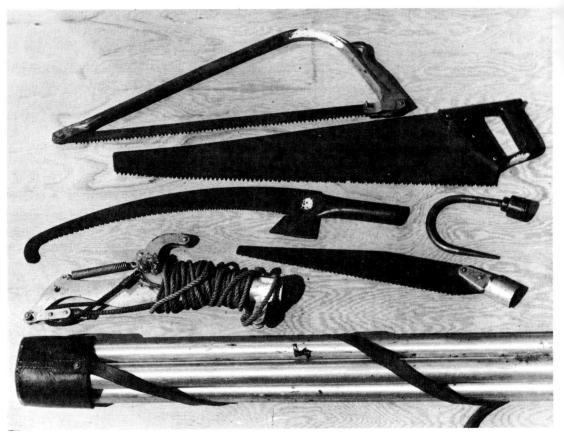

7 Range of hand saws and pole saw attachments

Use of ladders

Most care should be exercised when erecting and lowering ladders. The larger pull-up type will need at least two experienced operators. All three sections are stood against the tree, the top section is pushed or pulled up to the maximum and then the second or middle section is erected taking the top section with it. The base of the ladder should be firmly positioned and be situated approximately a quarter of the height of the ladder from the base of the tree. Removing the ladder is a simple operation. Before leaving the ladder, the climber will tie a line to the top rung and pass it over a branch and back down to the ground man. Then, by holding the rope and lifting the base, the ground man can safely lower the ladder to ground level.

The majority of good-quality ladders have a stop to prevent over-extension and at least three rungs will overlap. If there is no stop, it is perhaps safer to leave an overlap of four rungs.

There is a tendency not to use ladders at all. The climber will use other climbing aids, ie climbing irons or free climb. This should be controlled very carefully to avoid the abuse of irons and the increase in risk to the climber.

As already mentioned, ladders are normally used

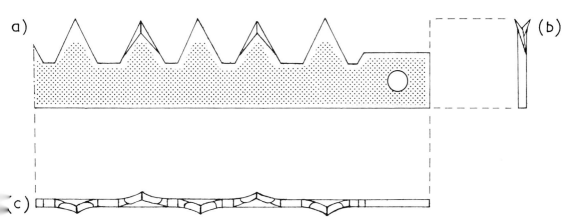

Fig 5　Fleam tooth crosscut saw
a　Side view of teeth
b　End view of set
c　Plan view of set

a)

(b)

c)

only to give access into the tree and therefore need not be tied in. However, there are certain operations where the climber may wish to use the ladder in conjunction with a harness and line. Non-professionals will use a ladder as a working platform, and in both cases the ladder must be tied in securely. This is achieved by tying a short rope to the top rung, round the branch or trunk and back on to the rung with a clove hitch.

There have been many nasty accidents caused by the improper use of ladders. Three particular examples are: (i) resting the ladder outside the cut; (ii) not allowing sufficient ladder above the branch to allow for the upward movement of the branch once the end has been cut off; and (iii) cutting off the end of a branch without under-cutting so that the branch tears and swings back towards the operator.

If the base of the ladder is stood on concrete or other smooth surfaces, the stiles should have wooden or rubber stops. Sections of a ladder should not be lashed into a tree, nor should they be stood on movable objects such as lorries or trucks.

Care and maintenance of ladders

With careful handling, aluminium ladders should require very little attention. They can be stored on top of the transporter. However, if they are damaged they cannot easily be repaired and the whole section may have to be replaced.

Wooden ladders need very careful attention. A continuous watch should be kept for any signs of cracking, loose rungs or rot. They should be cleaned periodically and then treated with linseed oil. They should never be painted as this will hide defects. Broken or loose rungs can be replaced but this must be done by the manufacturers. Some companies offer a very good maintenance service. Wooden ladders should be stored under cover and off the ground, with the weight taken off the bow.

Steps, trestles and scaffolds

There are situations where ladders cannot be used. Hedges and young transplants will not support the weight of a ladder and operator. On certain jobs, eg tying-in or netting large fastigiate conifers, lightweight scaffolding can be used. Although this may take time to erect, it is probably the best and safest way of tackling the job.

Hand Tools

Mechanisation has replaced many of the fundamental hand tools in tree surgery. The axe has been reduced to log-splitting and grubbing roots and the two-man crosscut saw is now only a museum-piece. Both these tools were the essential working tools of the game and men took great pride and care in their use and maintenance. Jim Beeching, before he retired as one of the country's leading tree surgeons, told of his early days when they would have up to a dozen large crosscut saws at any one time, each set for a different type of wood. On his retirement Jim Beeching presented Merrist Wood Agricultural College, Surrey, with many of these old saws and a range of early chain saw models. These will form part of a tree-surgery museum which the college hopes to develop. The development of the chain saw has changed many techniques as well as making many hand tools obsolete. The increase in costs and higher wages has made the use of high-maintenance tools questionable if there is a suitable alternative.

The main hand tools are described below, but the more specific hand tools for bracing and cavity work etc will be detailed later.

Hand saws

Despite the development of chain saws, there is still the need for a range of hand saws for tree-surgery work. There are three main types used (7): crosscut saws, small pruning saws, and pole saws.

Crosscut saws

The most common use of a saw in tree work is to crosscut green wood. Therefore, it is important to select a saw designed for that purpose. The fleam tooth pattern is ideally suited and is fitted to both the bow saw and the conventional carpenter's hand saw (fig 5).

Larger branches will be cut with a chain saw, so it is not necessary to select hand or bow saws of any great size. Commonly used sizes are the 600mm (24in) hand saw or the 525mm (21in) bow saw. Opinions differ as to which is faster or gives the better cut. Both can be purchased at various sizes of teeth. Teeth are measured by the number of points per 25mm (1in) of blade length. The greater number of teeth results in smaller teeth and a finer cut. The size normally preferred for tree work is 5½ points per 25mm.

The main advantage of the bow saw is the replaceable, maintenance-free blades. Although they are the same shape and size as those of a hand saw, the teeth on a bow-saw blade are hardened and will have at least three times the life of the teeth of a conventional saw. When blunt they can be replaced. This saves time and money.

Hand saws need regular sharpening and occasionally they will have to be jointed (stripping

down the teeth to one level) and then re-cut and sharpened. This is a highly skilled job and if it is not done properly the saw will not cut correctly. It may be possible to have this done by the manufacturers.

Another important aspect of cutting is the degree of set on the teeth. To prevent the saw from binding or running heavily, the saw kerf should be a little wider than the thickness of the blade. This is achieved by bending the teeth alternately to the right and to the left. Hard woods will be cut best with a fine set whilst soft woods need a fairly wide set to help clear the sawdust (fig 5). Hand-saw teeth can be set with setting pliers whilst with bow saws it is perhaps better to have a range of blades, set fine and coarse, and to change the blade when and if necessary.

Small pruning saws

A great range of small pruning saws are available and many have the Grecian pattern teeth that cut with the pull and are particularly suitable for cutting above the head. This type of saw is not used extensively by the tree surgeon but it has its uses for larger shrub and fruit tree pruning.

Pole saws

The pole saw is basically a pruning saw on an extended long handle. It is of great use in tree work for reaching out to cut small branches and when cutting from ground level or from an hydraulic platform. However, it can be abused. Operators can work a long way from the cut and take a very long time. With modern safety harnesses the climber can get well out on branches.

There are various types of pole saw. Perhaps the best is the 'Park Pruner' which consists of $4 \times 1 \cdot 6$m (5ft) poles and pruning saw head and a lopper head (plate 7). All are jointed with a firm screw thread. Fibreglass sets are also available. These are used extensively by electricity board staff because of their non-conductivity but are rather brittle and will break if dropped any distance.

Maintenance of saws

Apart from sharpening and setting, hand saws should be kept clean and rust-free and stored well clear of ropes and harnesses. Spare locking nuts for securing the blade to the handle on hand saws and spare rings for attaching the blade of the bow saw should be carried in stock.

Other cutting tools

A range of rough-cutting hand tools are used on occasions. Axes, mattocks, hooks and slashers are

8 Small axes, loppers and secateurs

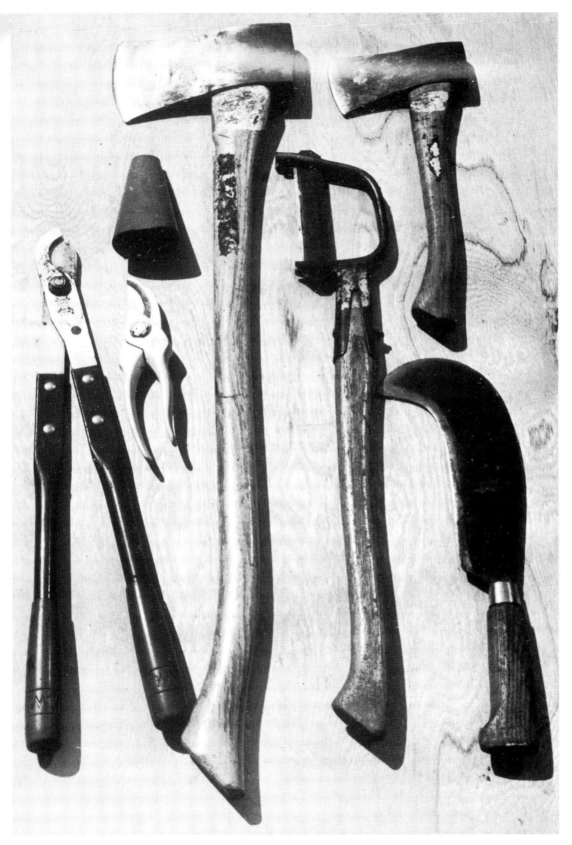

9 Trewhella 'monkey' winch showing anchor
tree protection

used for rough cutting jobs, ie grubbing roots,
clearing, hand hedge work and cutting up brushwood for burning and loading (8). Select a size
suitable to the operator and keep sharp and
rust-free.

Loppers, two-handed pruners and secateurs are
particularly useful for shrub and fruit-tree pruning,
and a good strong pruning knife should be carried
by all tree-surgery staff for paring cut surfaces and
detailed work (8).

Cleaning tools

All units should carry rakes, brooms or besoms for
clearing up after work. A client may be as impressed
by the neat finish as by the most skilled and
complicated tree-surgery operation.

Specialised Hand Tools

Hand augers, chisels, mallets, wire cutters and
draw vice tensioners will be dealt with under
Bracing in Chapter 8, and cavity cleaning tools and
equipment in Chapter 9, under Cavities.

Small Mechanical Tools

This particular section of this chapter will be out
of date very soon, for it seems as though almost
monthly there is some new machine or model on
the market. After many years of making do with

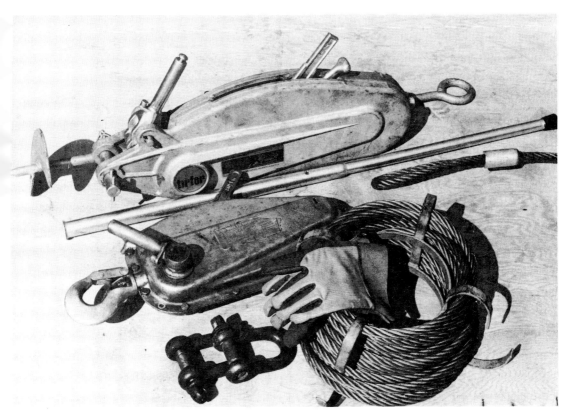

other industries' tools, at last manufacturers are realising the market potential and are developing new tree-surgery equipment.

10 Range of Tirfor winches and ancillary equipment

Hand winches

Many operations can be made safer and more efficient by the use of portable hand winches. Most types can be taken by hand to almost any situation, and the pulling and lifting capacity of the operator can be increased dramatically. Two commonly used types are discussed: the Trewhella 'Monkey' winch and the range of Tirfor winches.

Trewhella 'Monkey' winch (9)

This winch has served many industries and offers a very strong, portable system that is particularly useful for large tree-pulling and stump-removal. The winch is designed to be operated by two men, and no more than two should be used. One important safety feature is that if two men put the load on to the winch, two must release it. Pulling direct from the drum the winch exerts a 5 tonne (ton) pull. When used with a snatch block and grab this load can be doubled to 10 tonnes.

The winch is mounted on small wheels and is too heavy at 85kg (185lb) to be carried any distance. In fact, the complete outfit consisting of winch and lever handle, drum rope, pull rope, snatch block and grab totals 188kg (412lb).

43

If handled properly, this is a very useful and powerful portable hand winch.

Trewhella also manufacture a 'Monkey' jack, a very useful lifting tool – but again heavy.

Tirfor winches (10)

Three models are available in the Tirfor range: the T.7, TU.16 and T.35. The T.7 is very small and is not considered here.

The TU.16 is a very light portable hand winch which weighs only 18kg (40lb) and has a safe working load of 1600kg (32cwt). Its use is limited to light work but many small, awkward jobs can be managed by this model. As it would not be difficult to overload the winch, there are three brass shear pins in the base of the forward gear lever. If the safe working load is exceeded these will break and the load will be maintained. The machine can be reversed safely, the load lessened and the shear pins replaced. Spare shear pins are housed in the carrying handle.

The T.35, the largest of the Tirfor range, has a safe working pull of 5 tonnes. This winch will tackle all but the heaviest of jobs and is still portable enough at 29kg (59lb) to be carried by one man. No more than two men must operate the winch with the lever handle provided. This handle must not be extended beyond its designed length. There are no shear pins on this model.

Operational safety points of hand winches

It is very important that winches are thoroughly maintained and serviced by qualified mechanics. All accessories such as slings (chains should not be used), cables, shackles and snatch blocks and grabs must be greater in strength than the winch, as the winch has built-in safety features. All accessories should be maintained as the winch. Never exceed the safe working capacities of the winch or exceed the manpower pull as specified.

If the pull point is high in a tree the winch will rise off the ground when under tension. This is

12   Modern light and medium weight chain saws

11   Early wheeled chain saw with butterfly chain

perfectly safe but care must be taken if the load is suddenly removed as the winch will drop to the ground. If the winch is being used to pull over trees, the winch must be further away from the tree than its height.

Anchoring systems

In many situations a neighbouring tree can be used as a secure anchor for winches. It must be checked to see that it is stronger than the tree being pulled over and it should not be a smooth-barked type that will easily be damaged. Whatever the tree, care should be taken to protect it. Anchor trees can be protected in many ways. Whatever system is used it must be adequate to prevent damage and portable so that it can be readily carried to the site. A simple system is as follows.

On rough-barked trees short lengths of cord wood, 1m long × 75–100mm dia, packed inside the anchor sling should be adequate (9). If the tree is still liable to damage, sacks can be filled with twigs or brushwood placed between the tree and the cord wood. All but the sacks can be cut on site. When winching, check that the anchor sling is not riding up the cord wood or the cord wood cracking.

If there is not a convenient tree, other anchoring systems can be used. A range of manufactured anchors are available through the winch suppliers. For light work the winches can be anchored to a lorry towing hitch or tractor and the wheels chocked.

Chain saws

The modern chain saw, with its attachments, has done more than any other tool to alter methods and to increase efficiency. With the great range of types, sizes and attachments available there are very few cutting jobs that cannot be carried out with chain saws.

As with any other comparatively new tool, not all users have been properly trained and many accidents have occurred. In many eyes chain saws are still very dangerous tools and their use limited. Some even prohibit their use whilst climbing.

Types, sizes and selection of chain saws

The most common type is that powered by a direct drive two-stroke petrol engine. Other power systems that have specific uses are hydraulic and pneumatic.

The developments and improvements in chain saws over the past few years have been dramatic. From heavy, slow-cutting, unreliable saws which virtually vibrated themselves and the operator to pieces there is now a vast, sophisticated range of tools for every situation (11 and 12). The major improvements have been in the speed of cutting

and the reduction of weight and vibration. The noise problem is still there and must be the next subject for consideration by the manufacturers. Some have already reduced noise without any real effect on power.

There are so many makes and models available that selection becomes difficult. The following points should be considered.

SIZE REQUIRED The size of the engine and length of guide bar required will be determined by the use of the saw. The following sizes are available (i) Light: 30–44cc engine, 3–4kg (7–9lb) total weight and up to a 400mm (16in) guide bar. Used only for light work, easily abused by heavy cutting. The saw for climbing operations. Has replaced hand saws for all but lightest work (12). (ii) Light-Medium: 50–60cc, 5–7kg (10–13lb), up to 610mm (24in) guide bar. A useful size as can be used at height and being more robust can cut larger wood and do light felling. (iii) Medium: 60–80cc, 7–8kg (13–16lb), up to 710mm (28in) guide bar. General-purpose saw for forestry work, thinning, felling and cross cutting (12). (iv) Heavy: 90–130cc, 8–12kg (16–24lb), up to 1,020mm (40in) guide bar. For large felling and cross-cutting. The two-man types have been virtually replaced by the largest one-man saws.

SUPPLIES, SPARES AND SERVICE After selecting the size or sizes required, it is important to investigate the proximity and reliability of stockists for the supply of the unit, the availability of spares and the efficiency of servicing if required. It is difficult to keep comprehensive spares and not all operators are skilled mechanics. If a saw is to be efficient, it must be available for use at all times and this will be the philosophy of good agents.

USER PREFERENCE Some users may keep to one make with its range of models for all their chain-saw requirements. This may ease the spares problem and staff will be familiar with daily maintenance routines. Some, because of previous experience, have a particular like or dislike for a particular make. Staff should be prepared to investigate new types if they have obvious advantages. Many saws have attachments which may give the saw additional uses.

COST If, after the above three considerations, there is still a choice, then value for money must be considered. The cheapest or lightest may not be the best. Even the most expensive may be value for money if it gives reliable service.

Use of chain saws

Chain saws are potentially very dangerous tools. In both experienced and inexperienced hands accidents occur. The only statutory regulations covering chain-saw use are those in the Agriculture

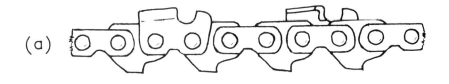

(a)

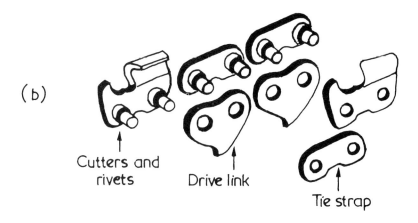

(b)

Cutters and rivets   Drive link

Tie strap

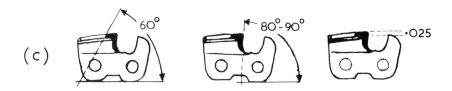

(c)   60°   80°-90°   ·025

(Field Machinery) Regulations, 1962. Although these regulations apply only to employed staff in agriculture and forestry, the standards they set should be followed by all. The main requirement is that one-man chain saws must be fitted with either a guard between the handle and chain or a rigid bar which extends above and along the back of the saw for at least 230mm (9in). Two-man saws must be fitted with a rigid bar above and along the whole of the chain. In addition, every prime mover must be fitted with a device by which it can quickly be stopped. The purpose and method of operation of the stopping device must be clearly indicated.

The Power Saw Association of Great Britain (11 Park Mansions, Prince of Wales Drive, London SW11) has produced a *Code of Practice for Chain Saw Users*. This covers only ground work but is well worth reading.

Before starting the saw, operators should read the instruction book and familiarise themselves with the controls, the fuel mixture, and whether oiling is manual or automatic. The fuel tank should be filled with the correct mixture and the

Fig 6   Chain saw chipper chain
a   Detail of chipper chain
b   Exploded view of links and rivets
c   Filing angles

Fig 8   Chain saw maintenance tools
a   Bar groove scraper
b   File holder
c   Parallel round file
d   Depth gauge jointer
e   Flat file

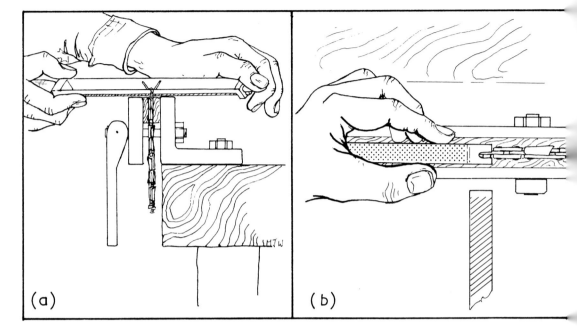

(a)
(b)

Fig 7   Chain maintenance
a   Sharpening in a filing vice
b   Plan view of filing depth gauge

chain oil tank filled with a non-throw chain-saw oil. The chain should be checked for sharpness and correct tension. Check that there is a statutory guard fitted between handle and bar and that the ignition switch is functioning. Operators should be properly attired (see Clothing for Tree-Surgery Staff, Chapter 3) and should ensure that there is no person in close proximity. If felling in woodland conditions, prepare an escape route and remove obstacles. Check tree for any foreign objects such as nails, wire, stones or soil.

Starting saws requires practice. The light types can be pull-started in the hands but larger models must be placed and firmly held on clear ground. When cold the engine will need choking. Once the chain is running the operator should check that it is being lubricated. New chains will need running in for five minutes with frequent oiling and adjustments to tension. Check idling control.

Cutting should be done at full engine revs. Cutting is irreversible, so the operator must check the line and be fully aware of the result of his actions. The weight of the saw should be on the felling dogs and the operator should only guide and pivot the saw. The saw will cut upwards from under the branch but the best cutting position is at the bottom of the bar as near to the engine unit as possible. If cutting logs on the ground, the

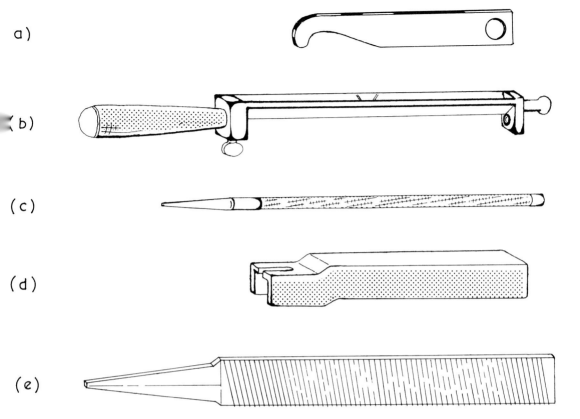

a)

b)

(c)

(d)

(e)

operator should cut through from the top. Care must be taken not to tip the chain into the soil and it may be necessary, therefore, to roll the logs over.

The operator must never transport, adjust or re-fuel the saw with the engine running. When refuelling, the operator must avoid spilling petrol on to the hot engine parts.

When chain saws are being used at height, the ground man should fuel, check and warm up the saw before passing it to the climber. The climber should use a chain saw only when in a safety harness or a pole belt or on a hydraulic platform. Great care must be taken to avoid cutting the life-line and branch ropes. Only experienced staff or trainees under supervised instruction should use saws at height. When not in use the saw must be turned off and suspended from a strop or attached to a line. The lightweight types are ideally suited to climber operation but on occasional large trees a heavier saw may be required.

Maintenance of chain saws

All machines require regular maintenance, and chain saws with their small two-stroke engines, cutting action and dirty working conditions perhaps need more than most. Regular and thorough maintenance is not only desirable but essential if reliability is expected. Operators

should have read the manufacturer's maintenance handbook.

DAILY MAINTENANCE Saws in constant use will require daily attention to the chain, guide bar and engine unit.

The modern chipper chain is made up of links and joined by rivets (fig 6). The cutter link is designed for cutting green wood and must not come in contact with nails, stones, or soil. Even with care the cutters will require perhaps twice-daily sharpening. To prevent filings dropping into the guide bar, the chain should be removed and placed in a filing vice (fig 7). The sharpening is relatively simple if staff are properly trained and equipped. It is necessary to maintain the correct angles on the cutter (fig 6). This can be achieved by using correct file and file holder. The size of the file is determined by the pitch of the chain. The pitch is ascertained by measuring between any three adjacent rivets and dividing by two.

Pitch of chain (inches)	File size (inches)
$\frac{1}{4}$	$\frac{5}{32}$
$\frac{3}{8}$	$\frac{7}{32} - \frac{3}{16}$
0.404	$\frac{7}{32}$
$\frac{7}{16}$	$\frac{1}{4}$
$\frac{1}{2}$	$\frac{1}{4}$

The Oregon file holder or the File-N-Guide

will hold the file and give the operator a visual guide to the correct angles. All top plates must be maintained at the same length, and if new cutters are fitted they must be filed back to the length of the existing ones. As the top plate is filed back the leading depth gauge should be lowered by using a depth gauge jointer and flat file (fig 7). The setting of the jointer is again determined by the chain pitch (check manufacturer's handbook for details of each make):

Pitch (inches)	Depth gauge setting (inches)
$\frac{1}{4}$	0.020–0.025
$\frac{3}{8}$	0.025
0.404	0.025–0.030

The drive links and tie straps will not need any maintenance but will indicate operational and maintenance faults by their wear patterns. Workshop power-sharpening systems are available and can be used in conjunction with, or instead of, the hand methods.

The friction generated by the chain running round the bar at over fifty miles per hour does cause considerable wear. Adequate oiling is essential and many guide bar and chain faults are caused by insufficient oiling. At the end of each working day the bar should be removed from the saw and the bar groove scraped clean with a bar groove scraper (fig 8). The oil entrance hole should be carefully cleaned. After a day's use there will be a build-up of burrs on the edge of the bar rails. These are removed with a flat file (fig 8). Sprocket and roller-nosed bars should be greased frequently. After maintenance the bar is returned to the saw. It is advisable to alternate the bar daily to give an even wear pattern.

If the saw is working satisfactorily the only daily maintenance required on the engine unit is cleaning and tightening nuts and screws. Cleaning is necessary to remove all dust and chippings from the moving parts and between the engine fins. The air filter should be cleaned thoroughly. There are many types of filters; the plastic, wire and nylon types can be cleaned in petrol whilst the paper or cardboard types are best blown clean with an air line and replaced regularly. A check to tighten all nuts and screws is essential to prevent parts vibrating and breaking. The nylon starter pulley cord should be checked for signs of wear and replaced if necessary.

PERIODIC MAINTENANCE Depending upon use, the saw should receive workshop maintenance perhaps weekly or every two weeks. Checks should be made on the wear patterns on chain, bar and sprocket. If sharpened properly, chains will give many weeks of use, but eventually they will need to be replaced. Every time a new chain is fitted the sprocket should also be renewed. Many operators run two chains per saw to save the cost of a sprocket and will, therefore, always have a spare sharp chain.

The guide bar should last the life of several chains, but checks should be made to see if it is still serviceable. The bar must be flat and with no signs of blueing or cracking. The bar groove depth and width should be measured, as the rails will wear with use.

The engine unit will require thorough cleaning and checking for cracks and defects. Spare spark plugs and points should be carried and fitted when necessary. Mechanical repairs should be carried out by qualified mechanics.

Hydraulic and pneumatic chain saws
Pneumatically powered chain saws have been available for many years and are used particularly for underwater work. Their application has always been very limited in tree work because of the size of compressor required to power the saw. With the advent of new pneumatically powered hand-held cavity cleaning tools, their use may be more widespread.

Hydraulically powered chain saws (13) and attachments are comparatively new in this country and have a very useful function, particularly when used in conjunction with hydraulic platforms when they are light, powerful, quiet saws needing little maintenance apart from that normally carried out on chain and bar. Their use must be limited to trees to which vehicles have access. The models so far available in this country are still not large enough to manage heavy felling or cutting operations and their cost by comparison with direct-drive petrol types is still high.

The chain saw can be extended on a pole to give extra reach and manoeuvrability.

Chain saw attachments
Many chain saws have attachments which will give versatility of use and mechanical aid to operations previously hand-powered. Most of these attachments can be fitted quickly by the operator. The following are available.

AUGERS (as seen on page 100) Used for tree feeding, cavity work and cable and rod bracing.
HEDGE CUTTERS Particularly useful on the lightweight range of chain saws.
CAVITY CLEANING TOOLS (as seen on page 98) Powerful, robust tools, very useful for large open cavities.
CLEARING SAWS The conversion from a chain saw to this clearing saw takes a little longer than

other attachments but gives a very useful tool for clearing undergrowth and small trees.

STONE CUTTERS For allied industries, ie landscape work. Can cut stone, brick and other similar materials.

Other small mechanical equipment

Now that tree surgery is established and developing, a more realistic market potential can be seen by manufacturers. There are already a number of mechanical tools and this range is bound to increase over the next few years. As already mentioned, many of these tools are also available as chain saw attachments. The following are either available or in an advanced state of development.

Augers and drills

Both petrol-engined and electric types are available. The electric drills are used for cable-bracing and test-boring. They can be powered direct from the mains through extension leads or from a portable generator. Electric tools should not be used in wet conditions.

Hedge-cutting tools

Again available with petrol engines and electric power. Larger types can cut through thick branches and are particularly useful for large-scale operations.

Hydraulic tools

Once the tree work unit has hydraulic power, the range of tools could be very extensive. Already available are loppers, clearing saws and drills, and cavity cleaning tools are being developed (13).

Pneumatic tools

Like hydraulic tools, those powered by compressed air are quiet and powerful and have low maintenance costs. The small hand-held cavity tool is already in an advanced state of development, and other tools should be developed in the future.

Sprayers

Not used in this country to a great extent, but have many applications in general arboricultural work. The powered knapsack sprayer is portable and can be used for fungicides, insecticides and herbicides. Great care should be exercised when using chemicals, and readers are advised to consult the Approved Chemical list issued by the Ministry of Agriculture. Other chemicals used in arboricultural work, eg growth inhibitors and anti-transpirants, can also be applied by sprayers. Whatever chemical is used, the tank and spray nozzles must be cleaned thoroughly after use.

Large Mechanical Equipment

The range of large, specialist tree-surgery equipment is increasing, particularly from America. Whether or not to acquire one or more of these expensive tools is a very important management decision. Many of the main items listed below are available from various manufacturers. When deciding which to buy, thought should be given to the supply of unit, spares and service; reliability; adaptability; and cost comparison.

Hydraulic platforms

The versatility, range of sizes and ease of use of hydraulic platforms have been realised by many industries. However, very few tree surgery units, apart from major local authorities, are using them and are perhaps dissuaded by the apparent high purchase price. In many situations, particularly street tree maintenance, the initial cost could soon be returned by reduction in labour costs; more important, non-climbing staff can be employed.

A range of sizes is available and the transporting vehicle will vary in size depending on the maximum height of the platform. One of the main advantages in urban areas is the use of quiet hydraulic equipment including chain saws. Most types have dual controls so that the ground staff can lower the operator in an emergency. Many adverse weather conditions that make normal climbing hazardous or impossible need not be a problem if staff can get to all parts of the tree in the platform bucket. There are, however, many situations where limited access will prohibit the use of such units, and on soft ground the vehicle may become insecure even with stabilising jacks. The safe carrying capacity of the bucket should never be exceeded and a special watch should be kept for overhead power lines. Highly insulated versions are available for 'hot-line' electricity board teams.

Stump-cutters

There are many ways of removing stumps (see Disposal of Stumps, Chapter 10), and one of the most efficient is to employ a stump-cutting machine. All makes available in this country are manufactured in the United States of America. Few companies or local authorities would have sufficient use to justify the purchase of one of these units, but several firms offer them for hire with operator. Quotation prices will vary with the number of stumps and distance from base but prices are competitive and may well prove to be the most cost-effective method of removing stumps.

Stumps should be cut as close to the ground as possible with a chain saw and the machine will chip the remaining stump down to a depth of up to 600mm (2ft).

A range of sizes is available from 1m (3ft 4in) to 2·5m (8ft) access clearance. All are towed by a vehicle and whilst some work from the power take-off of the towing vehicle, others have their own power units. These machines are noisy, and operators are advised to wear goggles and ear defenders.

Brushwood-cutters

Many operators, particularly those in urban areas, have a brushwood disposal problem. Fire lighting may be prohibited and transporting brushwood any distance becomes a very expensive operation. The large brushwood-cutters may solve this problem by reducing the brush into chips. As much as one fifteenth reduction in volume is claimed and this will minimise transport costs. Again, only large units will have sufficient use to purchase a brushwood-cutter, but short-term hire can be arranged through the United Kingdom agents.

The machine can be adjusted to take up to 200mm (8in) dia wood, but at this setting the chips will be too large to be of use as a mulch. Many uses have been sought for the chips, but the main saving of the machine is the reduction in transport cost and the use of chips should not be a major consideration when deciding whether to purchase.

The noise generated by the unit could well prohibit its use in certain areas. Operators should be properly trained in the machine's use and provided with goggles, gloves and ear defenders.

Combination units

Units combining an hydraulic platform, brushwood-cutter, hopper and transporter are also now available from the USA. As tree work develops, as it has in America, it seems likely that such specialised street tree maintenance units will be used more in this country, particularly if climbing staff are not available.

Forestry and land clearance equipment

Many large items of equipment such as tractors, half-tracks, tracklaying vehicles, timber lifting and loading equipment are used for large-scale tree-clearance operations, but are not considered here. Many tree-surgery companies would normally hire a specialist sub-contractor for such operations with specially trained and equipped staff. The tractor and lorry mounted powered winch is a very useful tool, particularly for felling operations. The fast retrieve pull of the power winch will aid directional felling much more than hand winches. Only staff experienced in their safe and proper use

should be allowed to use power winches. The 'Hyab' lorry-mounted type crane is also useful for log lifting, and larger units are using these successfully.

Transport

Most tree work units will need mobility, and some thought should be given to selecting the right type and size of vehicle.

The combination unit has already been described and is of a more specialist nature. The choice normally is between van, Land Rover and lorry. If a small van is selected it should be large enough to carry the team and all their equipment. Such a vehicle cannot, of course, carry any brushwood or cord wood from the site and a second vehicle will have to be used if this has to be cleared. Those who select a lorry will have the extra cost of purchasing and running such a large unit, and if it is over 3 tonnes the driver will need a Heavy Goods Vehicle licence. The Land Rover is a very versatile vehicle with its four-wheel drive and the ability to carry small hydraulic platforms and/or tow a trailer for carrying brushwood or cord wood.

Areas should be provided in the vehicle for the proper storage of equipment. Ropes and harnesses must be kept clear of cutting tools and chemicals. All tools must be held securely in place during transit. For safety, reliability and appearance the vehicle should be kept clean and well maintained.

Stores, Workshops and Garages

Throughout this chapter the need has been stressed for regular and proper storage and maintenance of tools and equipment. Space should be provided for the proper storage of tools and equipment both in the unit's vehicle and at the base or depot. Ropes should be suspended in a frost-free, well-aired space, clear of cutting tools and chemicals. It is perhaps best to have a separate storage space for equipment making it easier to check missing items. Missing tools are not only a financial loss but could create a danger if left in a public area. Storage areas should be burglar-proof and advice should be sought on fire prevention and control. No more than 22 litres (5 galls) of petrol should be stored without properly constructed fuel storage tanks.

Most units will require workshop facilities, particularly for chain saw maintenance and wet-weather work. The chain saw workshop will require benches, vices and chain-filing vices, chain breakers and rivet spinners and, if preferred, a motorised chain-sharpening system. · Shelves, drawers or boxes will be required for storage of spares.

5 Materials and Chemicals

A great range of chemicals is available to prevent or control pathogens, to accelerate, inhibit or prevent growth and to reduce transpiration. It is not intended to detail insecticides, fungicides or to any extent herbicides in this book. Further details of these chemicals can be obtained from the advisory leaflets and bulletins published by the Ministry of Agriculture and the Forestry Commission, the *Weed Control Handbook*, Vol 2, 7th edition (Blackwell: 1972), and the *Insecticide and Fungicide Handbook*, 4th edition, (Blackwell: 1972).

Luckily, this country has never carried out mature tree spraying operations on ornamental trees as is practised in some countries. Only recently have chemicals been used to any extent in an attempt to control the ravages of Dutch elm disease. This has been carried out, in the main, under controlled scientific study. There is, however, always the risk that with such an epidemic some will use highly toxic substances without due care and attention or even the knowledge of what harm they could be doing. Under the Pesticides Safety Precaution Scheme, the manufacturers concerned agree not to market any new chemical until recommendations for safe use have been agreed with the government department concerned.

Many of the materials discussed are harmless but it is as well to treat all chemicals as being potentially dangerous and the following points should be adhered to:

1 Read labels or instructions carefully.
2 Use products as recommended and at the correct dilution rates.
3 Safely dispose of all used containers.
4 Never transfer chemicals to other containers.
5 Keep all chemicals locked and well clear from children and animals.
6 Close tightly any partly used containers.
7 Avoid drift or spillage of chemicals.
8 Wear protective clothing as recommended.
9 Wash thoroughly all containers, sprayers, protective clothing and exposed parts of the body after use.

Wound Sealants

The bark of the tree insulates the active inner tissues, protects them from the elements and prevents the entry of pathogens. Any wound will expose these active tissues and they will be damaged or destroyed if not protected. A wound sealant or tree paint is applied to exposed surfaces and acts as a temporary bark. The British Standard 3998, *Recommendations for Tree Work*, refers to a fungicidal sealant but does not define what it should contain. A sealant should be non-toxic, malleable, long-lasting and easy to apply. The colour is also of some importance.

Sealants are sold as liquids in cans or bottles. The following proprietary brands are available.

ARBREX AND ARBREX 805   These are bitumastic sealants that have been used extensively for treating wounds. Arbrex 805 contains a copper fungicidal additive and can be regarded as a fungicidal sealant as defined in BS3998. Available in 1 gall (4·5 litre) containers for professional use and in smaller cans for garden purposes, it is manufactured by Pan Britannica Industries Ltd.

ARBORSEAL   A bitumastic sealant that is sold in 1 gall (4·5 litre) cans. It does not contain a fungicide, and is marketed by Honey Bros Sales Ltd.

BITUPROOF III   A general-purpose bitumastic paint used in general industry as a waterproofing agent. Now being used successfully as a tree paint, it is non-toxic and if bought in quantity – say 175 litres (40 galls) – is the cheapest sealant available. It is manufactured and marketed by Shell Composites Ltd.

It is possible to tone down the stark black of the bitumastic types by mixing with such products as Green Aqua-seal.

SANTAR   This is a paste containing 3 per cent mercuric oxide, used particularly on fruit and ornamental tree pruning cuts to help healing and prevent canker. It is, therefore, a fungicidal sealant but is sold in glass jars which are not very convenient and is expensive. The grey colour blends in well with bark. It is marketed by Duphar-Midox Ltd.

LAC BALSAM   A wound dressing manufactured in Germany. It contains a callus-inducing hormone and appears to have lasting and expansion qualities equal to the bitumastic types. Its olive green colour is very good and will help camouflage large wounds. Its cost is still high. It is marketed in the United Kingdom by International Tree Services NV.

Wood Preservatives

Wound sealants are necessary to protect living tissue, but when major areas of heartwood are exposed – especially if diseased – a wood preservative may be used. Care should be taken not to apply the preservatives to the living tissue as it may be damaged. This is easily overcome by painting living tissue first with a wound sealant. The purpose of applying the wood preservative is to control any fungal organisms and prevent the entry of others. A number of wood preservatives can be used but one specific product is *Xylamon Arbor*, marketed as Lac balsam

Growth Inhibitors

The regrowth of suckers on trunks, particularly after heavy pruning, can cause annoyance and expensive maintenance. These can be removed mechanically but good results have been achieved by painting or spraying the trunk with a growth inhibitor or regulator. The effect is to reduce the amount and vigour of regrowth, thereby reducing the problem. Maleic hydrazide is the chemical used, and the only product marketed for trees is Burtolin from Burts and Harvey (see Pruning Operations: *Unwanted regrowth*, Chapter 7).

Stump-killing Chemicals

It may be necessary to treat tree stumps with chemicals to prevent regrowth. Stump-killing chemicals are highly toxic to all plants and great care must be exercised to prevent damage, particularly to neighbouring trees. Details of the safe methods of applying those chemicals are given in Chapter 10. Commonly used chemicals are ammonium sulphamate and sodium chlorate. Ammonium sulphamate is a highly soluble, translocated and soil-acting herbicide. It is non-toxic to animals and non-flammable but corrosive to metals and should be applied only from stainless steel or plastic containers. Sodium chlorate is a translocated soil-acting herbicide, available as sprays, dusts or soluble granules. Proprietary brands should contain an additive to reduce risk of fire.

Cavity Filling and Covering Materials

The advantages, disadvantages and methods of filling cavities are detailed in Chapter 9.

Filling materials

Fillers should have the following qualities: (i) flexible to movement of the tree; (ii) contain no toxic substances; (iii) durable enough for the length of time required; (iv) easily applied; and (v) easily removed.

The following materials are used:

WOUND SEALANTS AND SAND These can be mixed into a stiff paste and if supported can give a malleable filling material, particularly for basal and pocket cavities, and can be removed fairly easily for re-inspection of the cavity. A mixture of sealant and sawdust is not recommended as this will dry out and break down.

CEMENT AND CONCRETE FILLINGS These are still recommended in BS3998 for basal filling but they cannot add any strength or support to the tree and are extremely difficult to remove for essential maintenance of the cavities.

PO COMPOUND A malleable plasticine-like material used for filling small cavities. It is particularly useful for plugging test bore holes and small depressions. It can be removed easily.

RIGID FOAM FILLERS These have been experimented with over the past few years and do offer a quick, effective and easily removed filler for cavities of any size or shape. Polyurethane and Urethane have been used. Both are supplied as two liquids. When mixed a chemical reaction takes place and the liquids expand and set into a rigid foam. The speed of expansion and setting is dependent on air temperature and, in any case, this must not be below 10°C (50°F). The trials so far indicate that the Polyurethane foams tend to retract and draw away from the cavity walls, thereby allowing water and organisms to gain entry. This has not occurred with the Urethane types and the early conclusions tend to favour this material. Both will require some harder surface to prevent bird, animal and vandal damage. Plastic car body fillers have been used with some success.

Covering materials

Covering of cavities is described in Chapter 9 as an alternative to filling.

FINE WIRE MESH This can be tacked round the cavity opening and painted. Expanded metal, used as a reinforcement material, is often used successfully.

FINE PLASTIC NETTING Although this covers equally well, it would be easily damaged by birds and animals.

GLASS SCRIM This has been used by some for lining large uneven cavities; if hardened with a quick cure resin, it can provide a very satisfactory covering material.

SOLID TIN PLATE Covers or caps are not so easily handled and are perhaps too obvious when used in a tree.

Anti-transpirants

Although primarily used during tree transplanting and production, there are occasions when there is a need to reduce transpiration during tree work operations. If roots are damaged or if large areas of the bark are removed by mechanical damage or vandalism the effects of this will be reduced if the leaves are sprayed with an anti-transpirant.

Synchemicals S.600 is a polyvinyl-chloride liquid which, when diluted with water, is sprayed on to the undersides of leaves to block the stomata temporarily, thereby reducing transpiration. Similar products are Clarital, supplied by Applied Horticulture Ltd and Scandiaseal from Scandinavia Nurseries Ltd.

6 Preparatory Operations

Once properly trained and prepared with a knowledge of the structure and growth of trees, of the effects of pests and diseases, and of the legal implications of his work, and provided with the correct tools, equipment and materials, the tree surgeon can commence work.

Many of the operations described in the following chapters are necessary only very occasionally, but as trees are removed or destroyed by development it is becoming increasingly important to safeguard and repair important specimens. This may be very expensive work, but what is the monetary value of an amenity tree? The operations carried out for the sake of public safety are necessary only where there is public access. There have been examples of unnecessary tree surgery in inaccessible woodland areas and this has brought forth the justifiable wrath of the conservationists. Nevertheless, where the trees are in public areas and are of landscape value, tree surgery is not only justifiable but highly desirable.

Seasons for Tree-surgery Operations

Contrary to popular belief, most tree-surgery operations can be carried out at all times of the year, bearing in mind the safety factors associated with adverse weather conditions. There are, however, some notable exceptions to this generalisation, itemised in Table 5.

Table 5: Seasons for tree-surgery operations

Operation	Seasonal exceptions	Reasons
Pruning: all cutting operations	Acers and Betulas should not be cut during very active sap periods, ie February to May	Will bleed profusely, therefore application of sealants difficult
	Juglans should be pruned only when in full leaf	Will bleed at all other times
Cleaning out and dead wooding	Carried out all the year round but dead wood easier to see when tree is in leaf	
Bark wounds and cavity work	Carried out all the year but avoid heavy frost conditions	Frost damage to exposed tissue
Cavity filling	Rigid foam fillers require air temperature of above 10°C (50°F)	Will not activate below this temperature

Operation	Seasonal exceptions	Reasons
Bracing and propping	Carried out all year but allow for weight differential due to leaf mass. Avoid high winds	Difficult to tension properly
Tree feeding: slow release granular types	Apply in spring, early summer	Active period of tree and root growth
Foliar feeds	When in leaf	
Tree felling, stump removal and timber clearance	Carried out all year round when ground conditions are satisfactory	Damage to seasonal attractions of shrubs and ground flora. Damage to soil
Tree inspections	Advisable to inspect twice annually, summer and winter	Summer leaves may indicate symptoms and in winter a more detailed inspection of the branch structure can be carried out
Pest and disease control	All seasons	Control will be determined by habit of pathogen and method of control

Characteristics of Trees

The characteristics of a tree may well affect the method of carrying out tree-surgery operations. Before commencing work the operator should be aware of any peculiarities and take the necessary action. Every tree is an individual and will present different situations or problems. Some of these peculiarities are potentially dangerous and note should be made of the following.

Brittleness of branches

Certain species of tree have very brittle wood, especially when green. The operator should be aware of these and make necessary adjustments. Genera that are a particular problem in this respect are ash, redwoods, some willows and horse chestnuts.

Quick-rotting wood

Certain trees are more prone to wood-rotting

organisms and, once infected, very soon lose their natural strength by the spread of the rotting agents. Most trees are liable to attack from wood-rotting organisms, but the following are a particular problem.

Horse chestnut timber rots extremely quickly after initial infection and all cavities or rots will need frequent inspections Limes and elms, particularly after heavy pruning, are liable to form cavities in the stumps if not treated Mature beech and birch will not respond to crown reduction and serious rot can set in. Oaks, on the other hand, are slow-rotting and even dead branches remain very strong. The sapwood is more likely to rot and be destroyed before the heartwood.

Natural structural faults

Some trees, by their growth, create potentially weak structures. The ascending branches of beech and some fastigiate trees will leave water pockets and weak fork formations. Large, heavy spreading branches are very prone to the kind of damage caused by wind and snow.

Climbing

Even with the advent of hydraulic platforms, there will always be a need for experienced climbers. The development of safety harnesses over the last few years has made climbing not only safer but more productive, with both hands to the job. The types and uses of harnesses, life-lines and other climbing aids are described in Chapter 3, and the details of knots used in conjunction with the harness in Chapter 4.

Even with the rope and harness, the operator still needs to climb the tree to reach a suitable anchor point. This tree-climbing ascent can be dangerous and the operator needs to have some natural ability to climb and must not, of course, have a fear of heights – although a healthy respect is desirable! This ascent can be made safer by the use of ladders or climbing irons. If there is no branch within reach the climber can tie-in with a strop whilst throwing his life-line over the next branch. Some operators use a light-weighted throwing rope and with experience can accurately throw this line up through a suitable fork, then pull through the life-line. Once the life-line is in position, the climber can anchor the line to his harness and with the aid of a ground man can ascend safely.

When climbing, the operator should always check each hold. Trust should never be put in dead or rotten branches. Care should be taken with downward sloping branches or tight narrow forks where boots can get stuck. Climbers should never over-reach or attempt to jump. Only one hold should be changed at one time, ie hand or foot. The body should be kept off the tree to get full lever action from the arms and legs.

Climbers need to be physically fit. An unfit person will soon become tired and tiredness can very soon lead to accidents. Any disability or illness will also affect climbing ability.

Trainees should practise climbing only under supervision. A life-line should be put into the tree first until the trainee has confidence and is fully familiar with the harness and knots. Only simple trees should be attempted at first and progression to more difficult specimens should be permitted only on ability.

Many able climbers may well be nervous at first or after a period of non-climbing. This is a perfectly healthy reaction and is better than over-confidence.

Making and Treating Cut Surfaces

The bark covering roots, trunk and branches acts as a skin and if broken can give rise to desiccation of tissues by exposure and the entry of harmful organisms.

Many operations discussed in the succeeding chapters do include cutting the bark and exposing the inner tissues. This is unavoidable, but all cuts should be kept as small as possible and cut back clean to live healthy wood to encourage active callus formation. A continuous clean callus area should be cut round the wound. In theory, all cuts should be treated with a wound sealant. In practice, this is not really feasible and it is normal to paint cuts exceeding 50mm (2in) dia. This must not, however, always be taken as a minimum. This size could be comparatively large on a small or young tree, and if there were a number of 50mm dia wounds in close proximity the total exposed area could be of some importance. The operator will often carry his paint pot with him, and all cuts of significance should be painted.

7 Pruning

Objectives of Pruning

Trees growing in their natural state can manage without the help of man, and pruning and other tree-surgery operations are unnecessary. However, trees growing in unnatural conditions, particularly urban situations, and where there is public access need to be kept healthy and safe and eventually have to be removed. There are, therefore, many very good reasons for pruning trees. The main objectives are as follows.

1 The formative pruning of young trees to develop a well-balanced crown or any other desired shape.

2 To improve balance or shape of semi-mature and mature trees.

3 The removal of dead and dangerous branches and the removal of crossing branches to avoid chafing or breakage.

4 The thinning of the crown of the tree for one or more of the following reasons: (i) to lessen wind resistance; (ii) to allow more light and air in or through the crown; (iii) to counteract root damage or structural faults; (iv) to form and renew a dense crown after heavy lopping; (v) to lessen physical and visual 'weight'; (vi) to reduce leaf volume and therefore leaf nuisance; (vii) to ensure safety of public and property.

5 To remove lower branches to clear pedestrian or vehicular access or to improve views.

6 To reduce the overall width and/or height of the tree where it has outgrown its situation.

7 To repair storm damage or other broken branches.

8 To produce flower or fruit, if so desired.

Formative Pruning of Young Trees

One of the most important aspects of tree establishment is the correct pruning and shaping of the developing specimen. Training and shaping of trees should begin in the nursery. Depending on the method of propagation and the ultimate shape required, the trees must be grown in clean fertile soil, planted at the correct distances, supported and pruned.

Fruit trees and bush-headed ornamentals will require special formative pruning. Forest-type trees will normally grow into the natural shape and form, but it is important to ensure (i) formation of a straight, strong trunk; (ii) formation of a well-balanced crown; and (iii) retention of a clear central leader.

At the time of final planting the tree should again be checked and the following formative pruning carried out if required: (i) removal of broken, damaged and diseased branches; (ii) removal of competitive leaders or twin forks which could develop into a dangerous structure; and (iii) removal of weak or crossing branches, and sometimes of others to ensure a well-balanced crown.

Branch Removal and Flush Cutting

The method of removing a branch will vary depending on its size and the proximity of features or structures beneath. All branches must be cut flush to their source to avoid die-back and/or vigorous regrowth, and to improve appearance.

Branch removal

Small branches that can be held in the hand can be cut flush in one cut from the top. Larger branches, however, need different techniques. If the operator attempts to cut flush from the top without first removing the weight, the branch may tear when the main support wood is severed. If the flush cut is attempted from the bottom, the weight of the branch will jam the saw. It is, therefore, necessary to remove the main part of the branch first. This is achieved by making two cuts (fig 9). The *first* undercut is made a convenient distance from the trunk. This cut must not extend too far as the weight of the branch will close the cut and jam the saw. The *second* cut is made a distance further out along the branch and is cut down from the top parallel to the first undercut. The distance between these two cuts will depend on the size of the branch but is normally between 25 and 50mm (1–2in). Some operators base this distance on the branch diameter. When the second cut reaches the level of the first, the branch will break along the grain and fall cleanly without twisting or tearing. (A large branch can be shortened in sections by the same two-cut method.) The *third* cut will be flush to the trunk (14).

Obstructions beneath the branch will prohibit the straight dropping of branches, and other techniques must be used. One method is to remove the branch in very small hand-held sections and throw the pieces clear of the obstruction. Secondly, a more involved method is to support the branch with ropes and lower and pull the branch clear. A third technique, requiring a great deal more experience and knowledge of

Fig 9   Branch removal
a   First, under cut
b   Second, severing cut
c   Third, flush cut

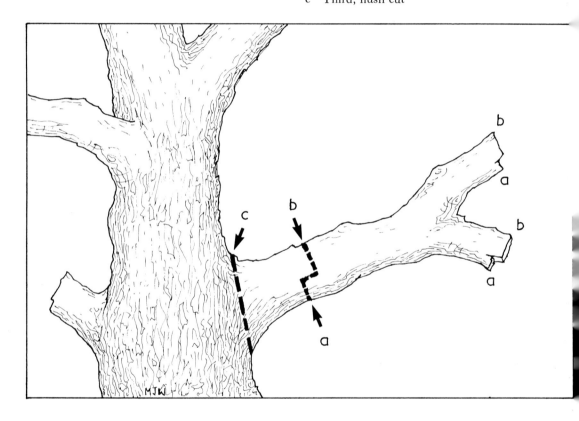

timber characteristics, is to cut a side hinge in the branch and pull the branch round through many degrees before it breaks and falls clear of the obstruction.

The removal of larger branches in small hand-held or guided sections is becoming more popular, particularly with the use of harnesses and small chain saws. This method should be used only by experienced staff and even then only when no really expensive damage can be done if an odd section were to fall.

The roping or slinging of branches is a time-consuming operation, but with the right ropes and staff quite large sections can be removed and lowered safely (15). The anchor or main support rope is put through a strong fork above the branch to be removed. The size of rope will depend on the branch weight. The positioning of the rope is important. The anchor point should be as directly above the branch as possible to prevent the branch swinging to its perpendicular. The point of the attachment to the branch will vary depending on the intended direction of fall. It is very difficult to estimate the exact balance point so that the branch will be suspended horizontally (fig 10). One way to counteract this problem is to remove the small end branches, so making it easier to estimate the balance point. Alternatively, two anchor ropes can be used and the branch cradled down. This is an extremely time-consuming operation and is seldom used.

The important point is that the operator should know which way the branch will go once cut. If there is any doubt, the branch should be cut off in smaller sections. Before cutting, a light rope should be tied to the branch to pull it clear of the obstruction when lowering.

The technique of pulling a branch round with a hinge cut is very useful when comparatively inexpensive obstructions are beneath the straight drop of the branch. A vertical wedge is removed on the side of the branch of the intended direction of fall (fig 11). A light line should be fixed further out on the branch. The operator then cuts through from behind the wedge leaving a hinge on which the branch will pull round before dropping well clear of the obstruction. This operation should be carried out only by skilled staff.

Flush cutting

Once the main weight of the branch has been removed, the final stump can be cut off flush with one cut from top to bottom without risk of tearing. If the branch base is approximately the same diameter as the branch, the stump can be removed truly flush to its source. However, many branches swell at their point of attachment to the trunk and

15 Branch removal with ropes over telephone line. Note traffic warning signals and barrier cones

Fig 10 Roping branches
a Strong anchor point
b Timber hitch at balance point
c Pull-off rope
d Branch rope securely anchored

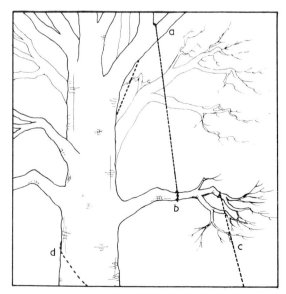

16 An example of flush cutting: top excessively
    rounded off with chain saw, lower cut
    adequately flush and more likely to callus
    evenly

Fig 11   Hingeing cut to avoid straight vertical fall
a   Hinge in direction of pull and fall
b   Back cut
c   Flush cut
d   Pull-off rope

if cut flush would leave a wound very much greater in area than the branch diameter. Such a branch stump should be removed at an angle from the top, attempting to minimise the final surface area yet not leaving a stump (16).

The increasing use of chain saws for pruning has exaggerated this problem, as it is so easy to cut too flush with mechanical aids. There is also an acceleration of the unnecessary technique of rounding off the final cut (16). This again increases the cut area and decreases the chance of healthy, even callus formation. The final cut must always be back into sound, healthy wood. Any rot or disease should be cleaned out and treated.

Paring of cuts

It is undoubtedly beneficial to pare the cut, particularly around the outer conductive and callus-forming tissues. This is done with a large, sharp pruning knife, leaving a smooth, even

surface all round the cut. In practice, this is rarely done in tree-surgery work and is necessary only where there is a very rough surface to the final cut.

Application of wound sealants

All cuts of any significance should be liberally treated with a wound sealant as soon as possible after cutting. Most operators will carry a paint pot with them and apply the paint immediately after cutting. Care should be taken to avoid pulling ropes over painted surfaces. If wounds are not painted at the time of cutting they should be done within the same day.

Pruning Operations

Over the years a number of terms have evolved to describe the objectives of pruning. In 1966 the BS3998 attempted to standardise the terminology used to describe these operations.

Fig 12   Crown thinning
a   Large tree close to building
b   Crown thinning to allow light to the building
c   Severe lopping temporarily removes problem
    but disfigures tree
d   Resulting regrowth after lopping and acute
    shade problem

Cleaning out

This operation consists of removing all dead, dying and obviously diseased or dangerous branches and stumps, the removal of fungal brackets, rubbish in forks, etc and any other unwanted items such as clamps, wires, nails and boards. Care should be exercised when removing embedded objects, as more damage can be inflicted. All *unwanted* climbing plants should also be removed. Whilst climbing, the operator will examine the tree for any defects such as cavities, water pockets, split and rubbing branches and other weak structures perhaps not obvious from ground level.

Crown thinning

Crown thinning is the reduction of the density of the foliage by first removing weak, thin and crossing branches and then such sound branches as necessary to achieve the desired reduction (fig 12). Crown thinning should be carried out at the branch tips, not by removing large, well-balanced branches from the main trunk. The ground staff should guide the climber as to the amount of thinning required on any one section of the tree in order to maintain balance.

Lifting of crown

Crown lifting or, as it is also known, raising the

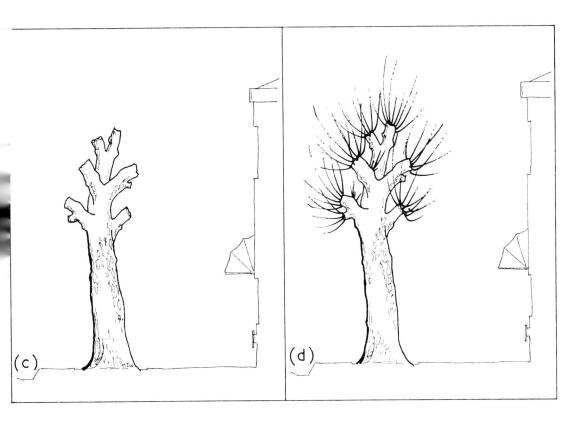

(c)

(d)

foliage, lift pruning or raising the canopy, is a comparatively straightforward operation of removing lower branches from the main stem or branch system to a specified height. It is carried out either to increase access or to improve views under the tree (fig 13). In its simplest form it is carried out on young trees to convert a feathered tree to a standard. On mature trees often very large scars will be left on the main trunk which may look unsightly and will require regular maintenance. This operation is not suited to many upright, formed trees, particularly conifers that look best with branches to ground level.

Reducing and shaping

Crown reduction, or, as it is sometimes unfortunately called, *drop-crotching*, is the reduction of the overall dimensions of the tree by shortening the branches back to growing points, leaving as natural a shape as possible. It is important to cut back to an existing growing branch so as to discourage die-back or vigorous regrowth from dormant buds and to improve appearance (fig 14).

Crown reduction is normally practised only on broad-crowned trees as it is difficult to retain a natural shape on fastigiate trees. Mature beech and birch do not respond to crown reduction and will die back from the cuts. This operation is usually necessary where the trees have outgrown their

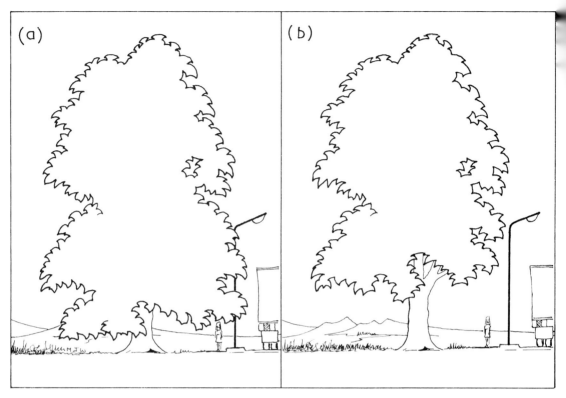

Fig 13　Crown lifting
a　Before; view and street lamp obscured, pedestrian and vehicular traffic hindered
b　After careful crown lifting

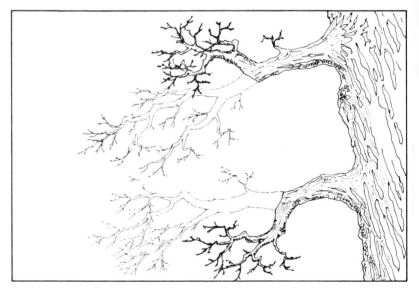

Fig 14　Reducing and shaping branches to reduce height and/or spread of tree. Cut back to growing point

17　Improper pruning operation: drastic lopping after large tree left too close to development

19 Dense regrowth problem in summer after pruning

18 Vigorous regrowth problem after regular lopping

Fig 15   Construction of retaining wall
a   Siting of wall in relation to crown and root
    spread
b   Detail of retaining wall

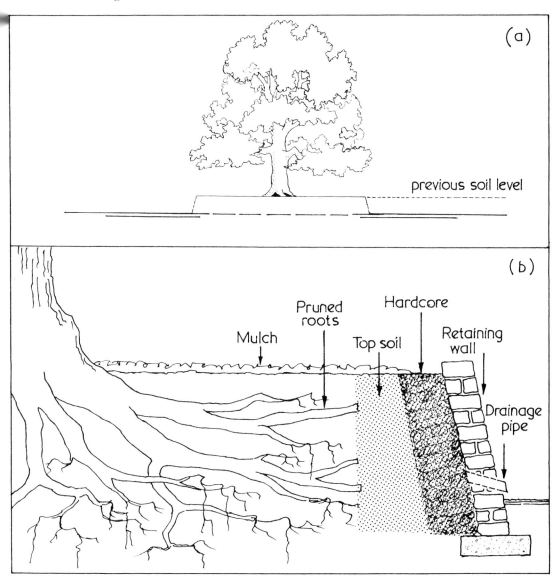

(a)

previous soil level

(b)

Pruned
roots

Hardcore

Mulch

Top soil

Retaining
wall

Drainage
pipe

situation and is done as an alternative to complete removal or the diabolical practice of lopping or topping (fig 12).

Crown renewal

Crown renewal is not a term used in BS3998, but it is covered in the overall term of *Restoration*. After trees have been mutilated by severe lopping or topping, often right back to the main trunk, many will produce vigorous regrowths from the stump and main trunk (17–20). If the original large cuts were improperly carried out or maintained they may well rot and the subsequent regrowths could be potentially very dangerous. Such trees should be very carefully inspected, and if the rots are extensive the whole stump should be removed, or, if feasible and required, the cavities can be cleaned and treated and the regrowths thinned and braced.

Street trees

Street trees that have been regularly pollarded to contain their growth can have their crowns renewed by careful thinning and shaping. The reasons for street-tree lopping are not always clear, or the original reason may have long been invalidated. Many of these old pollards may be well rotten and beyond repair, and perhaps the tree will be best removed and replaced. If, however, the stumps are reasonably sound, it is possible to renew the crown within a few years (20).

After one year's growth, the resulting shoots can be thinned leaving a balanced number per stump. These selected shoots are allowed to develop for a year or two until they require careful thinning. Within perhaps ten years a reasonable crown can be re-formed. Such re-formed trees will have a limited life, and this operation must be balanced against removal and replanting.

Unwanted regrowth

Unwanted regrowth may also occur on the main trunk and branches of trees after heavy pruning. These suckers or epicormic shoots are produced by dormant buds being forced into growth by the still active and full-size root system pushing the sap up to fewer normal top buds and leaves. Until the balance is restored these suckers will present a major maintenance problem if they are fouling access for pedestrians or traffic. Mechanical removal with saws or axes is possible but leaves ugly scars and needs to be repeated annually.

An alternative method of controlling these shoot is first to remove them and then, after painting the exposed tissue, to spray or paint the trunk with *Maleic hydrazide*. The effect of this chemical is to inhibit regrowth during the following growing season. The application rates depend on season Table 6 gives the timetable and dilution rates recommended by Burt & Harvey, the manufacturers of Burtolin, a growth inhibitor based on Maleic hydrazide.

Table 6: Timetable and dilution rates for Burtolin

Feb/March	April/May	June/July/Aug	Maintenance dose
1 part chemical	1 part chemical	1 part chemical	2½ parts chemical
2 parts water	3 parts water	4 parts water	8 parts water

Root pruning

If roots are exposed and damaged, they, like branches, should be cut off clean and smooth and painted with a wound sealant. It is not necessary to cut back to a growing point but it is essential to re-cover all exposed roots and paint as soon as possible. If a considerable percentage of the root system has been damaged, the safety of the tree must be established. If the surrounding soil level has been lowered, exposing the root system, it may be necessary to construct a retaining wall to hold the soil in place (fig 15). A retaining wall should be strong enough to withstand root growth and pressure and must allow for adequate drainage. Application of a granular fertiliser to the root feeding area may encourage fibrous root development. Severe root damage can to some extent be balanced by judicious crown thinning.

Maintenance of pruning cuts

When re-inspecting previously pruned trees, the original reason for pruning may no longer be valid. It is still important, however, to check all old pruning cuts and see if further work is necessary. All major cuts should be inspected for signs of rotting; even those completely callused over could be rotting beneath. After checking and cleaning, the cuts should be repainted. Callus formation around cuts should be even and regular. If there is no sign of callus formation on any part of a cut, this should be investigated and any dead wood removed and cleaned back to healthy tissue.

74

8 Preventative Surgery

Trees may have inherent weaknesses or develop faults that could affect their stability and natural strength. If these trees are of importance and the faults are recognised, tree surgery can be carried out to prevent further damage occurring. Many of these operations are expensive, by no means guaranteed foolproof, and their cost must be justified against the tree's importance and public safety.

Bracing

One of the main means of preventing trees breaking apart or branches falling is to support them with flexible cables or solid rods.

Recognition of weaknesses

To prevent damage, the faults must first be recognised. Many weaknesses are obvious and are comparatively easy to spot, whilst others need a more experienced eye or will be seen only by the climber.

Weaknesses that can be supported by bracing are as follows: (i) twin or multi-stemmed trees, particularly if tight forked (21); (ii) heavy and horizontal branches, especially conifers, which will collect snow and catch wind (22); (iii) where a branch or trunk has been weakened by cavities or storm damage.

Obsolete methods of bracing

These deficiencies and weaknesses have been recognised for many years, but some of the older methods of support either did not allow for trunk expansion or required regular and expensive maintenance.

One old method, often used on important village green type trees and carried out by the local blacksmith, was to bolt metal collars round the trunk and join these collars together with solid rods or chains (23). This effectively prevented the fork breaking but did not allow for natural tree growth. Within a few years the collar would constrict trunk expansion and cause actual damage. Not infrequently the constriction would cause die-back of the branch or even breakage. Some trees, however, outgrew the collar, and once the callus tissue joined over, the branch would continue with normal expansion. Many trees today still have these collars and it may be necessary to un-bolt or cut through the metal band to release constriction. To attempt to remove the collar could cause more damage. The rods that joined the limbs were inflexible and if chains were used these were unsightly and frequently broke.

In more recent times the metal collars were replaced by slats of wood and the chains by flexible cables. The cable is placed round the trunks and prevented from damaging the tissues by the protective wooden slats. This practice is very sound but still requires regular adjustment to prevent constriction as the trunk expands. Regular adjustment is not really a practical possibility on privately owned trees, and even on publicly owned trees is often overlooked. Many of these operations were carried out with excessively heavy cables secured with large shackles and grips and tensioned with turn buckles. This became a very clumsy and obtrusive practice and is rarely carried out today.

Modern technique of bracing

Since the 1950s many of the leading tree-surgery companies have developed techniques of bracing that are secure, unobtrusive, non-constricting and require little maintenance. There are now two distinct forms of bracing carried out by most arboricultural units: (i) flexible cable bracing with eye-bolts and/or screw-eyes; (ii) solid rigid bracing with tie rods.

1 Cable bracing Supporting branches with flexible cables is now a comparatively straightforward operation but does require specialist tools and equipment and detailed training in the many skills of positioning, fixing and tensioning the cables, the objective being to stop the outward movement of limbs but to allow flexibility.

Tools and equipment

CABLES Two main types are available and used. (i) *Galvanised round strand*, more commonly called multi-strand cable. A very flexible, strong and durable cable made up of six lays, each lay of nineteen individual strands, laid on to an oiled fibre core. Owing to its flexibility, it is very difficult to splice and needs to be fastened with bulldog grips (U clips) (24). (ii) *Galvanised mild steel seizing wire*, or seven drawn strand cable, is used to a limited degree but is less strong than the round strand type; therefore, heavier cables need to be used. It also stretches under load and this could result in slack cables. One of its main advantages is its ease of splicing which gives a very neat, trouble-free secure fixing (25). It is also cheaper, but as a heavier cable is needed to obtain

21 Obviously weak fork of twin-forked tree
    supported by cable brace

22 Modern bracing method supporting heavy
    horizontal branch

24 Detail of draw vice tensioning technique,
    cable secured by bulldog grips

25 Detail of eye-bolt, countersunk diamond washer and cable whipping

equal strength this is of little advantage. Table 7 compares the sizes and strengths of the two types of cable.

Table 7: Cable sizes and strengths

	mm dia	inch dia	Breaking loads (tonnes/tons)
Galvanised	5	$\frac{3}{16}$	1.36
round strand	6	$\frac{1}{4}$	1.92
	9	$\frac{3}{8}$	4.41
Galvanised	5	$\frac{3}{16}$	0.68
seizing wire	6	$\frac{1}{4}$	1.05
	9	$\frac{3}{8}$	1.78

The following British Standards give further details of the various cables: BS182, 183, 184: *Galvanised Iron and Steel Wire Ropes*; BS365: *Galvanised Steel Wire Ropes:* BS2763: *Steel Wire Ropes*; BS3530: *Small Wire Ropes.*

EYE-BOLTS AND SCREW-EYES The modern bracing technique is to drill holes into or through the limbs and fix an eye-bolt or screw-eye. The eye-bolt is a parallel bolt made from mild steel with a welded or moulded eye. The bolt is passed through the limb and secured by a nut, and the limb is protected by a diamond-shaped washer (fig 16a and illustration 25). The length of the bolt will be slightly more than the branch diameter to allow for tensioning. A range of lengths can be

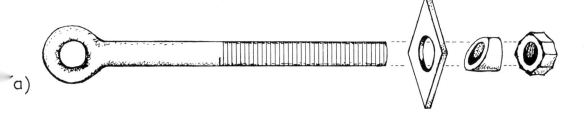

a)

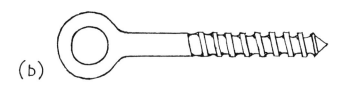

(b)

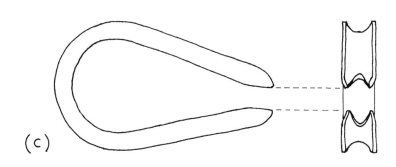

(c)

Fig 16   Bracing equipment
a   Eye-bolt
b   Screw-eye
c   Thimble
d   Bulldog grip

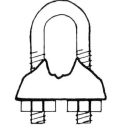

(d)

81

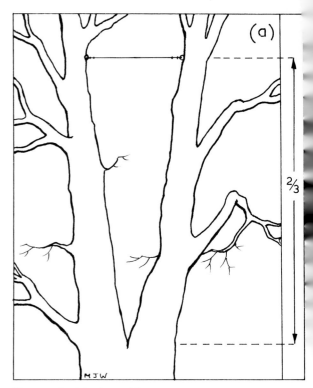

Fig 17   Positioning cables
a   Twin-forked or multi-stemmed tree
b   Horizontal branch
c   Detail of eye-bolt through branch ready for
     tensioning. Note angled washer

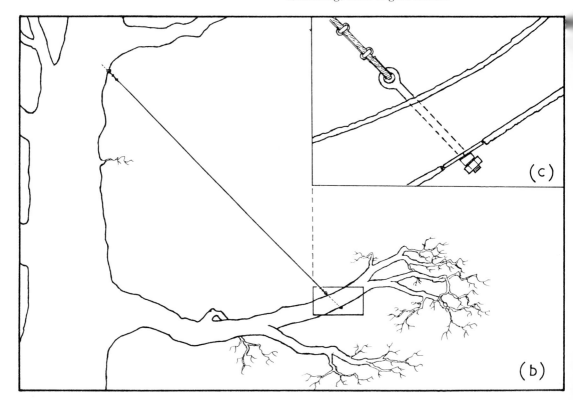

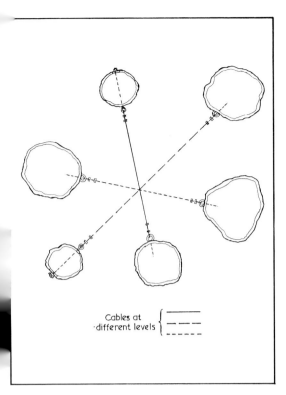

Cables at different levels {
— — —
- - - -
- - - - -

Fig 18   Plan view of braced multi-stemmed
tree – weak branch held with eye-bolt to
strong branch opposite

purchased. The diameter is normally 12mm ($\frac{1}{2}$in). The hole in the diamond-shaped washer needs to be greater in diameter than the bolt to allow for different branch angles. An angled washer may be required to bring the nut true to the diamond washer.

Screw-eyes are tapered screws or coach bolts with a welded or moulded eye. The screw-eye is turned into the limb (fig 16b). The lengths of screw-eyes normally used are 75mm (3in), 100mm (4in) and 125mm (5in); the top diameter would be 6, 9 and 12mm respectively.

THIMBLES When securing either of the two cables it is necessary to place a thimble between cable and eye to prevent chafing and damage. The thimble must be of the same size as the cable diameter and held securely in place by the cable fastening (fig 16c). Stiff galvanised thimbles are used, and a slightly more expensive type is the cadmium-plated brass thimble which is softer and much easier to use (see BS464: *Thimbles for Wire Ropes*).

BULLDOG GRIPS The galvanised round strand cable needs to be fastened by the use of bulldog grips or U clips (fig 16d). Again these must be the same size as the cable, and normally two grips are

used approximately 50–75mm (2–3in) apart (see BS462: *Bulldog Grips*).

SPECIAL BRACING TOOLS Hand or power augers will be required to drill the holes for eye-bolts and screw-eyes. These must be the right size for the job and kept sharp. The powered auger certainly speeds up the operation, but for small jobs and in difficult situations the hand auger is particularly useful.

Chisels and mallets are needed to countersink the diamond washer. A 37mm (1$\frac{1}{2}$in) carpenter's chisel is normally used and a rubberised mallet (which has proved to be more durable than the wooden types) can be used to drive in the bolts.

Pliers, wire cutters and spanners are required and should be of adequate quality and the right size.

Draw vice tensioners are used, particularly when using screw-eyes to tension the cable. These are used by electricity boards for cable tensioning, and the small sizes, 200mm (8in) overall length, are particularly helpful for bracing (24).

Once supplied with all these small items, some form of bag is required whilst working at heights. No bag is designed for this purpose but use can be made of ex-army shoulder bags or they can be made to specification. They should be deep enough to carry bolts, chisels, augers, etc.

Positioning of cables

The positioning of the cable is very critical and great care must be exercised if the brace is to be at its most effective (figs 17 and 18). In most cases, especially when supporting a weak branch to a strong one, only one brace is required. In both the forked tree and heavy horizontal branch the main principle is to support the weak branch as far out or as high as possible but still in strong enough wood to take the weight of the branch and the tension of the cable without distorting.

In the case of the upright fork, BS3998 states that the point of attachment is usually about two-thirds of the distance from the crotch to the end of the branch. The point of attaching the cable supporting a horizontal branch should be as high as possible so as to give an angle of not less than 45° from the weak branch. If the supporting branch itself is leaning towards the brace, it may be necessary to put in a second cable to counter-balance.

In a multi-stemmed tree each branch should be treated individually, and again the weak should be attached to the strong (fig 18). If more than one cable is to be attached to one trunk, they should be at least 300mm (1ft) apart. The old method of ring bracing (23) is not desirable, because if any one

Fig 19   Tie-rod

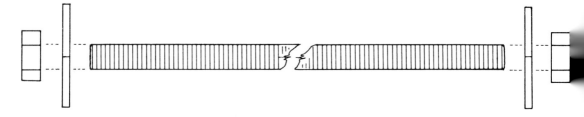

cable or rod breaks the whole system will be ineffective.

On very heavy branches or large forked trees it may be necessary to insert more than one cable. If this is done, two cables should not be fixed to one eye. This would mean that one cable must be out of line, and if this is slightly over-tensioned it could pull the bolt or screw down the grain of the wood and allow the entry of water and disease organisms.

Eye-bolts or screw-eyes?

Once the position of the cables has been decided the choice of whether to use eye-bolts or screw-eyes or one of each must be made. Eye-bolts are more expensive and take longer to fit but will give more support to a weaker branch and have built-in tensioning. Screw-eyes are comparatively cheap and very quick to screw into the tree. Their main disadvantages are that they may not be secure enough on a weak branch and there is no adjustment. On quick-rotting trees such as horse chestnuts, screw-eyes should not be used.

It is often a fair compromise to use an eye-bolt at one end and a screw-eye at the other, particularly when supporting a weak horizontal branch. Here it may be desirable to insert an eye-bolt through the weak branch to give a more secure hold and to use a screw-eye up in the main trunk. To use an eye-bolt on a large trunk would perhaps mean a very large bolt and a very costly operation for both materials and labour.

However, if fairly small upright forked branches are to be supported, it is quite feasible to use two screw-eyes and tension by some other means.

Fixing eye-bolts and screw-eyes

The eye-bolt will require a hole drilled through the trunk of the same diameter as the bolt. It is very important to ensure that the hole is in line with the intended cable run. It is difficult for the operator to drill and keep the line correct, so it is normal to have two climbers in the tree to guide each other. Once the hole has been drilled, the diamond-shaped washer is countersunk beneath the bark. If, because of the cable line, the bolt is

not at right angles to the trunk it will be necessary to insert an angled washer between the nut and the diamond-shaped washer (fig 17c). The bolt should be at least 50mm (2in) longer than the length of auger hole. When the bolt is inserted the eye should be left 25–50mm (1–2in) out to allow for tensioning.

Small screw-eyes can be turned into soft woods without pre-drilling, but with larger screw-eyes or on hard woods it will be necessary to drill the depth of the screw length, and the auger or bit should be 3mm ($\frac{1}{8}$in) less in diameter than the thickest part of the neck of the screw-eye. It should be difficult and stiff to wind in the screw-eye. A tommy bar or the draw vice handle can be used for leverage. It should be turned in right up to the eye.

Attaching cables and tensioning

If at least one eye-bolt has been used, the cable can be attached securely and tensioned as firm as possible by hand. If the round strand type is used the cable is secured with bulldog grips. These should be tightened securely, but not so tight as to flatten the cable, thereby breaking the galvanising and giving entry to rust. Two bulldogs are normally used, placed approximately 50–75mm (2–3in) apart. Cable ends can be cut to within 25mm (1in) of the bulldog, and for particular neatness this end can be seized to the cable by light whipping wire. The mild steel seizing wire can be secured by whipping. This is a very safe, neat fixing and takes no longer than fixing the bulldogs. Once the two ends of the cable are secured the cable can be tensioned by drawing the eye-bolt through the branch, tightening the nut against the washer.

If two screw-eyes are used there is no built-in adjustment and two other forms of tensioning can be used. One method is first to draw the branches together with blocks and pulleys, then, after fixing the cable, to release the rope, and it is hoped that the cable will be at the right tension. This method requires a great deal of skill and experience. A second, more commonly used, method is to tension the cables with a wire tensioner or draw vice. The

Fig 20   Tie-rod through weak fork

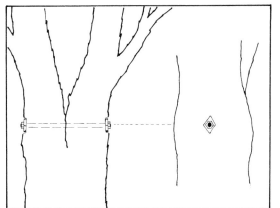

Fig 21   Tie-rod through cavity

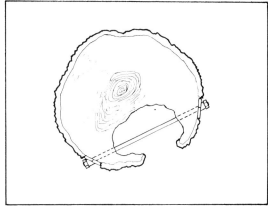

Fig 22   Tie-rod through split branch

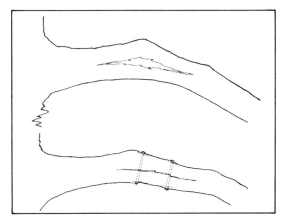

Fig 23   Tie-rod through crossing branches

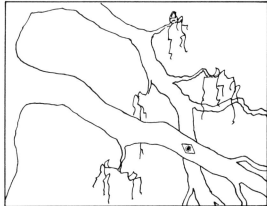

cable is passed through one eye and held loosely with a bulldog. The other end is fixed securely. The draw vice is attached to the same eye and the free end of the cable is attached to the draw vice. The draw vice can then be wound up until the required cable tension is reached. The cable is then firmly held at the other end and cut (24). Whichever method of tensioning is used, it is important to have the cable at the optimum tension to give maximum support. It is difficult to define correct tension; the cable should be as firm as possible so as to prevent snatching in winds,

but not so tight as to distort the natural tree shape.

Maintenance

The method of bracing with eye-bolts or screw-eyes has the great quality of being virtually maintenance-free. However, the feature that provided the original reason for bracing may deteriorate and at some time it may be thought wise to remove the weak branch or fork, or even the tree. Braces with bolts and screws have been used in trees for over twenty years, and if the original job was carried out properly, they can still

85

be secure. If the tree is in a public area or is one of particular visual importance it should be regularly inspected and maintained and the braces should be checked for security and effectiveness.

Limitations of cable bracing

Although many of the practicalities of cable bracing have been mastered, there are still some unanswered questions. What cable sizes and strengths are required when supporting very large trees? What are the forces and stresses in such a tree in high winds? These questions have never been answered adequately and there is a need for more research into these problems.

Metal and healthy wood are quite compatible and there have been very few instances of rot or breakage if the bolts or screws are inserted properly. However, there may be certain trees where perhaps they should not be used. A brace removed from a horse chestnut tree showed quite alarming staining and early stages of rot after being in place for only two years. Again, more research is required.

Does the owner of a tree that has been braced still face legal action if all or part of the tree falls? Has the owner in fact admitted weakness? It will be interesting if such a case comes before the courts.

An over-braced tree could be so inflexible that the whole tree would lever against the roots and could perhaps cause wind-throw or wind-break.

2 Rod bracing Solid rod bracing should never be carried out high in the branches as it would create an inflexible situation that would be potentially dangerous. There are, however, a number of situations where a solid tie rod can help support the tree and can be used in conjunction with flexible cable bracing or alone to support cavities, split branches, forks, etc.

Equipment

TIE RODS Tie rods, like eye-bolts, are constructed from parallel mild steel and have threads and a diamond washer at each end (fig 19). They can be of any length and are normally 12mm (½in) dia. The hole for the tie rod is drilled with an auger of the same diameter as the rod. The positioning of the rod will depend on the circumstances of use.

Positioning of rods

Rod braces are used in the following situations.

FORKED TREES These will be supported by flexible cable braces to prevent the outward movement of the limbs, and it may also be desirable to support the actual fork with rod bracing. One or more rods can be inserted through the fork, preferably at or just below the crotch (fig 20). The holes are drilled at approximately right angles to the trunk. The diamond washer is countersunk at each end and the nuts tightened (26).

LARGE CAVITIES These can be supported by tie rods to prevent splitting. A number can be inserted over the length of the cavity (fig 21).

SPLITS along the branch or down the trunk can be pulled together so as to induce natural healing by inserting one or more tie rods (fig 22). If there is an old split there may be internal rot and this will need treating as a cavity before bracing.

CROSSING BRANCHES These will cause rubbing and chafing and eventual breakage. Normally this can be corrected by removing the weaker branch, but if both branches are important they can be tied together so as to prevent rubbing and encourage natural healing (fig 23). Always check for internal rot.

Maintenance

Rod bracing should need little actual maintenance, and after the callus tissue has grown over the diamond-shaped washer it will be impossible to see. However, the feature that provided the original reason for bracing may have deteriorated and the tree should therefore be regularly inspected. If the tree eventually has to come down, the chain saw operator will need to avoid the braces in order not to damage his saw.

Limitations

The main disadvantage of bracing is that, unless carried out properly, it can give a false sense of security and the tree could still be dangerous.

Propping

Reasons for propping

Like bracing, propping is an operation carried out to prevent damage. Propping branches or trunks from ground level is necessary only when it is impossible to brace the tree in the normal way. The main reasons for propping are: (i) when there is no upper crown to brace to, eg trees like catalpa or cercis; (ii) when the upper crown is too weak to support forks or lower branches; (iii) when the whole tree is leaning or levering against the root system; (iv) where it would be unsightly to support low branches with cables.

Materials

NATURAL BRANCH PROPS These are the most

26 Bracing by tie rod through fork of twin-forked tree. After four years callus almost complete over diamond washer

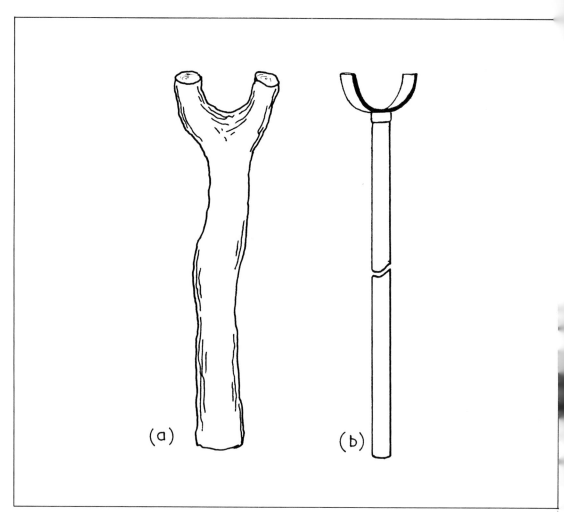

commonly used, and when felling trees a tree surgeon will often select suitable props for future operations. They should be selected from naturally durable wood, be straight-grained, have an open rounded fork and be of sufficient length (fig 24a).

CONSTRUCTED WOODEN PROPS It may be necessary to use these if natural branch props are not available or are of inadequate size.

METAL PROPS Props constructed from 50mm (2in) scaffold poles or box section with a welded cup are increasingly being used. The advantages are that they are very permanent and far less obvious (fig 24b).

Positioning of props

Props should be positioned where they will give maximum support and be as inconspicuous as possible (fig 25).

The most common situation where propping may be necessary is when there is no upper crown or a weak crown. Then the low, weak or heavy branches can be supported by props.

The prop is normally positioned upright from a firm pad on the ground to the branch. The fork or cup of the prop should be of roughly the same diameter as the branch. Some protection or padding will be necessary between the prop and the branch. Once the position has been determined, a firm base or pad needs to be created beneath the prop. This can be achieved by concrete, a paving stone set on hard core, or a metal pad. A prop of adequate size can then be offered up to the branch. To ensure a firm hold the branch can be carefully lifted and then lowered on to the prop. This can be done by jacking or winching. If this is carried out carefully, it should not be necessary to tie the branch to the prop. Care should be taken not to over-lift the branch, as this could put great stress on the branch and perhaps cause eventual damage.

Occasionally it may be desirable and possible to prop a whole tree. Small trees can be propped quite easily by angling the prop against the lean of the tree. Again, a firm base is essential.

One exceptional propping operation on a very

large cedar was successfully carried out by Beeching of Ash Ltd. The tree, which was leaning, was carefully winched back and a large, constructed wooden prop was put in against the lean. The tree was then allowed to settle back on to the prop. After several years the tree has still not moved any further and should have re-established its own anchor roots. This was a justifiable and not too obtrusive or expensive operation on such an important tree.

Maintenance

Wooden props will need to be inspected for rot or deterioration, and checks should be made to see if the prop is still adequate for the branch. If the branch increases in girth substantially, the prop may constrict growth and need replacing.

Limitations

The main disadvantage with propping is that it is obtrusive and difficult to disguise. Wooden props look more natural but are much heavier than the

metal types. Attempts to hide the prop with climbing plants may only draw the eye to it.

Fig 24   Propping materials
a   Natural wood prop
b   Metal prop

Fig 25   Supporting low heavy branch with natural prop

9 Remedial Surgery

Through many natural and unnatural causes trees may be damaged, weakened or just in general poor condition. If attended to in time these damaged or weakened areas may be treated or repaired, rots prevented and the tree made safer or its life extended. The justification for such operations will depend greatly on the amenity value of the tree, its rarity, historic importance and life expectancy. Due attention must also be given to public safety and, if the tree is of great importance, public access can be controlled by fencing. Many of the following operations can give a false sense of security, and major remedial operations should be carried out only by experienced and reliable staff.

Bark Wounds

The bark of a tree protects the inner conductive, support and growth tissues. If the bark is damaged or removed these important inner tissues will be open to the elements and to attack from a great number of pests, diseases and other troubles. The objectives of wound sealants and the treating of branch wounds have been discussed in earlier chapters but it is important to emphasise the need to treat and seal bark wounds as soon as possible to prevent further deterioration perhaps to major rots or cavities.

Causes

A great number of agencies can be responsible for damaging the bark; the following are common examples.

ANIMALS Grazing stock in particular can very quickly remove the bark and cause serious damage. The grey squirrel is now a major tree pest with its habit of removing bark from branches high in the crown, which results in die-back and stag-headed trees. Even domestic cats can cause damage by their claw-sharpening exercises and this problem is even more serious in safari parks where larger cats are free to use existing trees.

VANDALISM The bark is often removed at the base of trees, apparently without the knowledge that this may well kill the tree, and accounts for a great number of tree deaths. The carving of initials and graffiti on smooth-barked trees is more disfiguring than damaging.

FAULTY WORKMANSHIP Indirect damage caused by man is probably the most common and troublesome cause of tree injuries. Tree trunks appear to attract car bumpers, lawn mowers and a whole multitude of machines, equipment and substances on development sites. Even professional tree staff, using existing trees as winch anchors, may sometimes cause horizontal bruising and crushing which are very difficult to treat and slow to heal.

Effects

The effect of all this damage is to remove, crush or destroy the outer protective bark and expose the vulnerable inner tissues. If left untreated these wounds will attempt to heal themselves but perhaps not before the entry of wood-rotting organisms. Once established, these wood-rotting organisms can soon cause internal rots and cavities. The effect and speed of rotting will depend greatly on tree species.

Treatments

The best treatment is to prevent damage occurring, but however well we educate professionals and the general public, damage will always take place. Once the damage has occurred, it is important to treat the wounds as soon as possible.

All broken and bruised bark must be cut back to sound, undamaged bark. This is normally carried out with a 50mm (2in) carpenter's chisel or gauge and a rubber mallet. A strong pruning knife and paint scrapers are useful for detailed work.

It is desirable to cut the wound into a shape conducive to natural healing. Where possible the final shape should run with the sap flow (27–30). The edge of the bark should be at right angles to the wound. If the inner sapwood is damaged or splintered, this must be smoothed to avoid water-holding pockets.

A horizontal wound such as is caused by winch cables is difficult to treat, as to attempt to shape it into line with sap flow would mean considerable enlargement of the wound. There it is best simply to cut back to undamaged wood. Once the wound has been cleaned and cut to a suitable shape it should be coated with liberal dressings of wound sealants.

If young trees are severely damaged, they can be bridge-grafted to by-pass the damaged area. This is often done in fruit orchards after rabbit damage and could be applied to ornamental trees.

If the bark wound is older it may be necessary

to remove dead bark and any rotten wood before treating.

It is possible to prevent damage from animals by adequate fencing or guards and from grass-mowing equipment by guards or by keeping the grass clear of the tree trunk by mulching or using herbicides.

Maintenance

Annual or biennial checks should be made to see if the wound is healing properly, and if there are any areas where there is no callus formation the dead wood should be cut back again to live wood. All wounds should be repainted regularly.

Cavities

External damage and internal rots causing cavities probably have more serious effects on a tree's stability and safety than any other defect. The inspection, cleaning and treating of cavities is an operation requiring considerable expertise and experience. A thorough knowledge of wood-rotting organisms and their effect on different tree species is essential. The proximity of the trees to the public or to property are also major consider-ations. Even if treated, cavities must be regularly inspected.

Causes of cavities

All the agencies responsible for causing bark wounds will also be responsible for causing cavities if the original wounds are not properly treated. The entry and spread of wood-rotting agents will vary with tree species, but many will attack and destroy previously healthy trees as well as those weakened by other troubles. Some of the wood-rotting organisms can gain entry from root grafts from neighbouring trees, and serious diseases like honey fungus can remain alive in cleared land for many years and then attack newly planted trees.

The woodpecker is often accused of causing cavities, but in fact it will only peck into already diseased and rotting wood in search of insects or eventually to make nesting holes.

Unpainted pruning cuts and old branch stumps can lead to cavities, as can storm damage. Even apparently healed wounds are not necessarily safe and major rots can be hidden by the callus formation.

Effects of cavities

The effect of destroying the structure and wood of the branch or trunk is seriously to reduce its strength and to give rise to secondary effects of other harmful organisms. In natural woodland this is part of the life cycle with fungi living on the wood, insects using the diseased wood to breed and live, birds feeding on the insects, etc. In public areas this again is the ideal situation with the tree providing habitats for a great number of other life forms. However, if the cavity becomes of any size there is the very real risk of the branch falling or the whole tree collapsing. (Many of the trees blown over in gales will have some form of root damage or basal rots and cavities.) The tree surgeon can open up and inspect the cavities to see if the tree can be retained and then, if required, clean and treat the cavities.

Treatment of cavities

Cavities will need to be inspected to see how far they extend and to determine whether they can be treated or whether the branch or tree should be removed. If it is decided that the cavity can be treated the method will depend on its size and type in relation to the size and type of tree and the position of the cavity in the tree.

Cleaning

Whatever the size or proximity of the cavity, the first operation is to clean out all the rotten and visible diseased wood. This will often necessitate the removal of healthy wood to gain access (31). A lightweight chain saw is a useful tool for increasing access to a cavity either by removing old stumps or by enlarging the access hole.

Once adequate access has been achieved, it will be easier to judge the extent of the cavity and the safety of the tree. It is, therefore, advisable to carry out this preliminary work first in case it is then decided to fell the tree.

The removal of rotten wood back to sound, healthy tissue is a time-consuming and exacting operation and often very uncomfortable. A range of hand tools is available for this work. Carpenter's chisels, gauges, paint scrapers and rubber mallets are commonly used and purpose-made cavity tools can be purchased (32). A chain saw can also be used for cutting the rotten wood into sections. It is not, however, an ideal tool with its forward cutting action, and powered cavity-cleaning tools are now available (33). A torch, particularly one mounted on a safety helmet, is also a very valuable piece of equipment for working inside large, open cavities.

The cleaning of the cavity must be thorough, and if the rot is found to extend further than at first anticipated, again the safety of the tree may have to be questioned. The method of cleaning will vary depending on the shape and extent of the cavity.

30 Heavy dressing of wound sealant

32 Hand cleaning tools

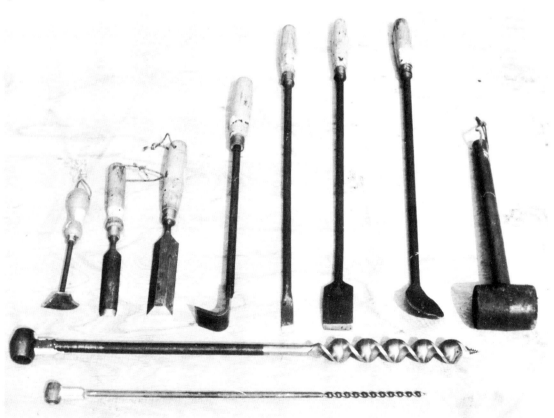

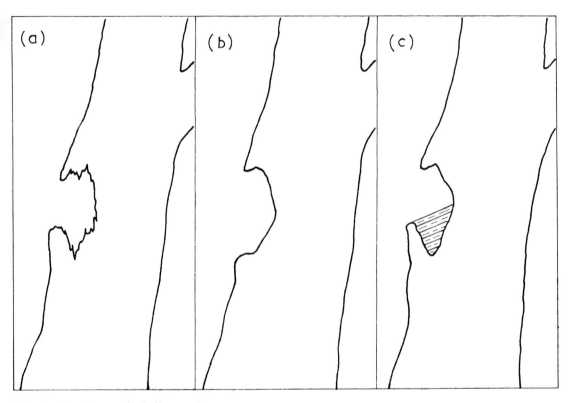

Fig 26   Treating small shallow cavity
a   Untreated cavity
b   Access opened and water-holding pocket
    removed
c   Access kept to a minimum and base filled

33   Powered cavity cleaning tool

34 Drilling drain hole for cavity treatment with
    mechanical auger

Fig 27 Treating deep cavity
a   Untreated cavity
b   Access increased, cavity cleaned, piped and
    covered

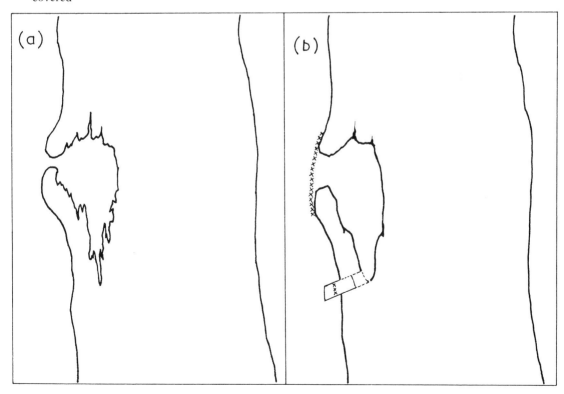

SMALL SHALLOW CAVITIES These are relatively easy to clean and the final shape should be conducive to natural healing and to the shedding of water (fig 26). Small cavities that extend deeper than the access hole can be cleaned out and a water-shedding shape achieved either by cutting out a V-shaped notch to the bottom of the cavity or by inserting a basal fill material.

LARGER DRY CAVITIES These should be cleaned in the same way. Again, it is important to enlarge the access hole so that cleaning can be carried out thoroughly.

LARGE DEEP CAVITIES CONTAINING WATER As extending the access sufficiently would remove a considerable amount of healthy wood and perhaps weaken the tree even more, these present a different problem. It is advisable to measure the depth of the cavity with a probe and then drill up to the base with an auger. First a small pilot hole is drilled. It can then be seen if the angle is correct. This hole is extended with a larger auger (34), preferably 50mm (2in). The water and accumulated rubbish can then be flushed through the hole (fig 27). Cleaning of this type of cavity can still be difficult, but the full extent of the rot can be determined.

BASAL CAVITIES As these may extend up into the heartwood, thorough cleaning may not be possible. As much rotten wood as possible should be removed to determine the extent of the rot and to see if the tree is still safe. Test boring at intervals around and up the trunk will help determine the spread.

Treating inner wood

Once the cavity has been cleaned out it may be advisable to sterilise the inner wood in an attempt to arrest the spread of the wood-rotting organisms. Wood preservatives are described in Chapter 5; cauterising may also be carried out with a blow lamp. In either case care should be exercised to protect the active sapwood.

Sealing

Once the cavity has dried out, the entire inner surface should be liberally covered with a wound sealant. Particular attention should be given to the outside wall of deep cavities and the auger hole.

Rod bracing

Large cavities can be supported by the insertion of tie rods right through the cavity. The number of rods required will depend on the size and position of the cavity (fig 21). Their function will be to hold the trunk together to prevent splitting. There must, however, be sufficient sound wood surrounding the cavity to give adequate support.

Final treatment

Small, shallow cavities and those with a water run-off should require no further treatment apart from regular maintenance. If a basal filling is required the materials described in Chapter 5 can be inserted after sealing. These basal fillings will hinder future inspections and this emphasises the need for easily removable materials.

If a drain hole has been drilled, it will be necessary to prevent callus forming at the lip, thereby blocking the hole. This is easily achieved by inserting a section of close-fitting pipe. Copper pipe is an ideal material, but expensive. Plastic waste or down pipe is a good substitute. The pipe needs to be inserted beyond the callus-forming tissue and should protrude only enough to prevent water seeping back into the hole (35).

The drain hole will allow free movement of water and air and, to prevent the accumulation of rubbish and the entry of birds and animals, the cavity access will need to be covered with fine wire or plastic mesh (35). Similarly, fine wire should also be placed in the auger hole. These final treatments are sufficient for all cavities, and if the mesh covering is fine enough and painted a fair degree of camouflaging will be achieved.

Cavity filling

The materials for cavity filling are described in Chapter 5 and their use is advocated for small basal fillings to achieve a water run-off. The use of materials for complete filling, however, must be questionable and their only real virtues are to camouflage or hide the large ugly scar on the trunk or to prevent vandal access to basal trunk cavities.

Filling must hinder re-inspection even if easily removable materials are used. It also gives a false sense of security by hiding the problem. The extra cost of filling can be justified only by the enhanced appearance of the tree, and it may be possible to achieve a comparable appearance by covering. However thorough the cleaning and treatment has been, it is unlikely that the rotting process will stop or even slow down. A fill material may well create dark, damp conditions that may accelerate the growth of wood-rotting organisms. If, however, it is decided to fill, the following techniques can be used.

RIGID FOAM FILLERS Probably the most easily used materials for large cavity filling, the major constraint being that the chemicals require an air temperature of above 10°C (50°F) to activate, restricting their use to a limited time of the year. The technique is still experimental.

35 Cavity in pollarded tree cleaned, drained, capped and covered

After cleaning and sealing the cavity a thick-gauge plastic or thin metal sheet is tacked or roped on to the access hole leaving a small aperture at the top. Slats of wood with nails half driven in may help speed up this part of the operation. With experience, the operator can gauge the amount of liquid required to fill the space. Two liquids are added together and on whisking a chemical reaction takes place and the mass expands and swells. It is critical, therefore, that the time between mixing and pouring into the cavity must be as short as possible. If the cavity is at height the ground man will pour the measured quantities into one container. This is pulled up by the climber and he stirs to increase the reaction and then pours the liquid into the base of the cavity. The top of the cover can then be tacked closed and the chemical allowed to expand and fill all the available space (36–41).

The foam will set hard within a few minutes; the warmer the air temperature, the faster the reaction and setting. Once set, the cover can be removed and the surface of the foam can be cut flush with a saw. The final surface will still be very porous and easily damaged by vandals, animals or birds. It may, therefore, be advisable to cap the fill with a stronger material. Trials with a car body filling kit have given very satisfactory results. Glass fibre and resin may also be used as a cover.

Finally the surface area can be painted with a wound sealant and made to look more natural by leaving a rough, bark-like finish.

CEMENT OR CONCRETE These substances should not be used for filling aerial cavities as even slight movement of the tree will allow air and water to enter between the cavity wall and the fill material, probably increasing breakdown of tissue. It is a misconception that concrete filling can add strength to a cavity. The only possible use of these materials is when basal cavities need to be filled to prevent the entry of vandals and animals and where the foam filler would not be strong enough. The cement has no strengthening or supporting properties. The major problem is the difficulty of removal for re-inspection or eventual felling.

Capping

Tin plate caps to prevent water access are occasionally used, but their appearance is ugly and their effect questionable. They do, however, prevent a build-up of debris in the cavity (35).

Maintenance

Cavities are formed by wood-rotting organisms, and however thorough the cleaning and treatment has been it will be impossible to remove or destroy all these organisms. They will continue to invade surrounding healthy wood and can be virtually undetectable without microscopic examination. It is essential, therefore, that all cavities should be regularly inspected and re-treated. At some stage the overall safety of the tree must again be questioned.

Water Pockets

Causes and effects of water pockets

Unlike cavities, water pockets are natural depressions formed at the base of ascending branches, particularly on multi-stemmed trees (fig 28). The effect of this pocket is to collect water and accumulated rubbish; the bark can be destroyed and a cavity may form. A cavity at a fork is potentially very dangerous and it is recommended to treat these pockets to allow free air and water movement.

Treatment of water pockets

The treatment of water pockets is similar to that for cavities containing water. An auger hole is drilled up to the base of the pocket and the rubbish and water are flushed out. After painting, a pipe is inserted into the auger hole and fine wire mesh or a cap is tacked above the pocket, to prevent the build-up of rubbish, leaves twigs, etc, and in the auger hole. These pockets should not be filled as rotting could take place under the fill without being noticed.

Maintenance

Treated pockets should be checked regularly to remove any build-up of silt and rubbish that may, in time, block the exit hole.

Storm Damage

The effects on trees of extreme weather conditions can be disastrous. Wind throw, where the whole tree and roots are blown over, and wind break, where the main trunk snaps, render the trees beyond repair. In less serious conditions branches may be broken off or split. Lightning can completely destroy a tree or, in certain circumstances, only superficial damage may be apparent.

After the storm has subsided, trees should be inspected for any signs of damage. Broken branches should be cut off flush and painted. Split branches may require rod bracing. If there are any signs of root lifting or any major damage to the main trunk the safety of the tree must be questioned.

Tree Feeding

Trees growing in natural situations obtain their

Fig 28 Natural water pockets in base of ascending branches

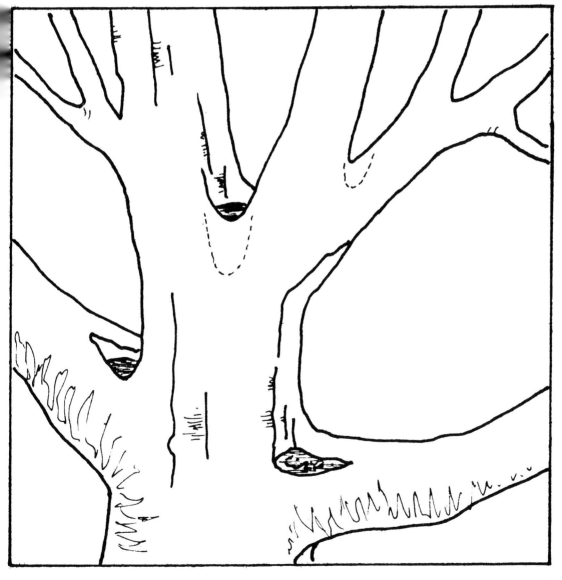

natural supply of nutrients from leaf litter which, when decomposed, returns essential elements to the soil. The woodland soil is also kept moist and insulated by the leaf layer. Natural soil life such as worms, insects, burrowing animals, bacteria and fungi help in the process by decomposing the leaves and making the nutrients available to the tree roots.

Many trees, however, are grown in unnatural conditions where fallen leaves are either swept up for appearance's sake or cannot reach the soil because of inpenetrable surfaces such as concrete, tar-paving or just severe soil compaction. Many trees growing in such conditions, particularly when mature, will show signs of nutrient deficiencies and steps need to be taken to ameliorate soil conditions to feed the trees.

Recognition of deficiencies

When trees are inspected or surgery work carried out, any symptoms of nutrient deficiencies should be noted and remedial action taken.

General lack of vigour and little or no growth in last season's shoots or branch increment indicate root damage or a lack of available nutrients. The leaves, being one of the most temporary parts of the tree, will indicate deficiency symptoms very quickly. Any leaves other than normal size or colour should come under close scrutiny to determine the cause of the deformity. Leaf nutrient-deficiency symptoms can easily be confused with other disorders such as those caused by fungi, bacteria, viruses, insects and a complete range of climatic, soil and environmental conditions. A detailed soil analysis can be carried out to determine the nutrient level, type and pH of a soil.

Tree feeding is not the cure-all that some believe, but it is important to recognise symptoms and to consider feeding whenever trees are treated.

Types of feeding materials

The type and quantity of feeding materials used will depend greatly on the condition of the tree and the access available. Specific deficiencies may be correctable by application of a single nutrient fertiliser, but often a more general type is used. The following are the most commonly used types of feeding materials.

Bulky organic materials

Well-decomposed bulky organic materials are a very useful commodity, supplying most of the major plant elements, and by their bulk they improve soil structure and drainage and retain moisture.

Well-rotted *farmyard manure* is a particularly useful material and if available at a reasonable price should always be considered. Decomposed *leaf mould* is the most natural way of returning nutrients to the soil and is often available from natural woodlands and by storing the swept-up leaves until decomposed. Other materials may be available locally, eg *spent hops* from breweries, *bark chippings* from timber mills and *seaweed.*

Bulky organic materials have many natural advantages, but consideration must also be given to possible drawbacks. First, access to the feeding roots may be limited or it may be undesirable to distribute large volumes of manure around the root system. Second, transport of the bulky materials is more difficult as such large quantities are required.

Concentrate fertilisers

Both organic and inorganic materials can be processed to supply plant nutrients. Specific fertilisers can supply individual nutrients, or when mixed a more general balanced feed can be applied.

Many of the commonly used fertilisers release the nutrients quickly, and the following mixture recommended in BS3998 has this main fault.

5 parts, by volume, ammonium sulphate (20% N)
5 parts, by volume, superphosphate (18% P_2O_5)
$1\frac{1}{2}$ parts, by volume, potassium sulphate (48% K_2O)

It is considered beneficial to select a slow-release fertiliser as a quick-release type may produce lush, soft growth that would be more vulnerable to pests and diseases and damage from adverse weather conditions.

Many proprietary brands of compound concentrate fertilisers are available supplying the major elements of nitrogen, phosphorus and potassium and some specific minor or trace elements. Types available in granular form have the added benefit of being easy to handle and store. Many also release the nutrients slowly. Although concentrate fertilisers do not have the mulching and soil-amelioration qualities of the bulky types they have the advantage of being easy to transport and store and can be applied direct to the feeding roots.

Liquid fertilisers

Liquid fertilisers can supply major and/or trace elements either to the roots or as foliar feeds. Drainage from large compost heaps can be re-applied to the tree's root areas. This is practicable only where large compost areas are stored such as major parks, nurseries or botanic gardens. Proprietary foliar feeds are available, but as well as being quick-acting they have the added disadvantage of being difficult to apply to large trees.

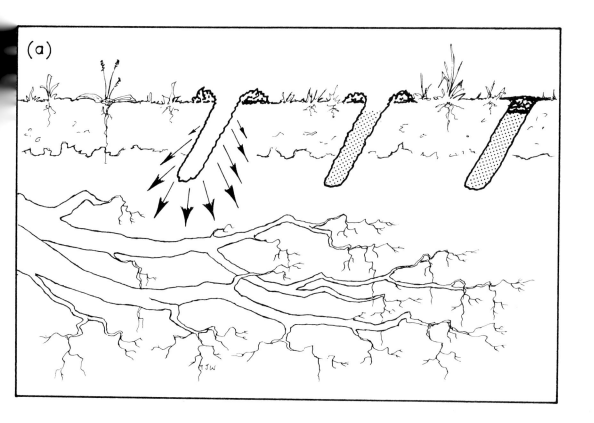

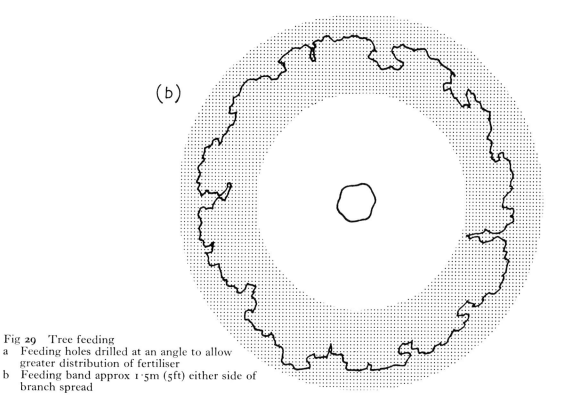

Fig 29   Tree feeding
a   Feeding holes drilled at an angle to allow
    greater distribution of fertiliser
b   Feeding band approx 1·5m (5ft) either side of
    branch spread

Concentrate fertiliser sticks

A comparatively recent introduction is the 'Green Pile' concentrate fertiliser stick. The main advantage is its simplicity. Each stick contains major plant nutrients and is simply driven into the ground around the root area. The stick is made of four layers of waxed paper, each layer containing a quantity of fertiliser, giving a 17 per cent nitrogen, 10 per cent phosphorus and 10 per cent potassium analysis. The fertiliser is released over a period of time as the layers of paper break down.

Methods of application

BULKY ORGANIC MATERIALS These can be applied to the root area, and normally this necessitates open ground beneath the tree. If the root area is covered by concrete, tarmac, gravel or even quality grass, bulky organics cannot normally be used. Turf can be lifted, the material applied, then the turf replaced. This is, however, a very time-consuming operation and rarely practised unless the tree is of importance.

When applying these materials, it is advisable to fork lightly over or aerate the soil beneath the crown spread. This breaks surface compaction and allows free movement of air, water and plant nutrients. The material is normally applied in a 3m (10ft) band, 1·5m (5ft) either side of the branch spread, and approximately 100mm (4in) thick. If in a dry state the material can be watered in, applying at least 10 litres/m² (2 gall/sq yd). The practice of removing top soil and forking-in the bulky organic material must be carried out with care as many surface roots may be damaged.

CONCENTRATE FERTILISERS It is possible to broadcast these over the root feeding area as above. The 3m band should be lightly forked over to break compaction and the fertiliser applied at 250g/m² (8oz/sq yd). The fertiliser is then watered in. The main disadvantage of this method is that surface-rooting plants, such as grass or ground-cover plants, may well utilise the nutrients before the tree roots.

A more thorough practice is to drill holes around the root feeding area and to insert the fertiliser into the holes, thus bringing it into more direct contact with the tree roots and away from the hungry roots of surface plants.

Again, it is common practice and recommended in BS3998 that the feeding band should be 1·5m either side of the branch spread (fig 29). Holes are drilled 300–600mm (1–2ft) deep and approximately 37–50mm (1½–2in) in dia. It is beneficial to drill these holes at an angle so as to allow greater surface coverage (fig 29). The holes are drilled at 450–600mm (1½–2ft) centres both in the feeding bands and between the bands. A power auger is the best tool for drilling the holes, although a hand auger or punch bar can be used. Another useful tool is a hand-operated bulb planter. A plug of soil is removed and the bottom extended with a punch bar. After applying the fertiliser the plug is replaced. Once the holes have been drilled the total amount of fertiliser to be applied to the tree must be divided by the number of holes to give the amount of fertiliser per hole.

The total amount of fertiliser given to a tree will be determined by the existing nutrient content of the soil and the age, size and condition of the tree. There has been little detailed research into this particular problem and only broad guidelines can be suggested. It is normal to apply 0·5–2kg (1–4lb) per 25mm (1in) of trunk diameter at breast height. Given a trunk diameter of 900mm and applying 2kg per 25mm, the total amount of fertiliser would be:

$$\frac{900}{25} \times \frac{2}{1} = 72 \text{kg}.$$

The number of holes drilled can be counted but a simple formula can be applied. If holes are drilled at 0·5m centres both in the bands and between the bands the formula is 19(4R+ 5), R being the radius from the trunk to the first feeding band. If first radius is 4m, the total number of holes on all six bands will be: 19((4 × 4) + 5) = 399 holes. Therefore, to calculate the amount of fertiliser per hole, divide the total amount of fertiliser into the total number of holes: 72kg ÷ 400 = 180 approx. grammes per hole. If imperial measurements are used and the holes are at 2ft centres and the first radius is 13ft, the formula is (13 + 5) × 19 = 342 holes. With a 36in dia tree and a 4lb per inch application the total fertiliser required will be 144lb. Therefore, the amount per hole is 144lb ÷ 342 = 7oz.

Once the amount per hole has been calculated, this quantity is weighed out and a convenient receptacle of that volume is used to apply the measured amount per hole. If the amount per hole is very small it may be beneficial to bulk it up with sand or fine peat so as to distribute the fertiliser evenly throughout the hole.

After application the feeding area is raked or brushed to backfill the drill holes and to leave the site clean and tidy.

Feeding by this method is very thorough but time-consuming, and if part of the root feeding area is inaccessible it is more difficult to gauge accurately the amount of fertiliser. The method also assumes that the majority of the feeding roots are in this 3m band either side of the branch spread. This is not a proven fact and observations suggest that this area may be too far out.

One other method of applying concentrate fertiliser is to excavate carefully fewer, larger holes or a trench and backfill with the required amount of fertiliser bulked up with sand, peat or compost. This encourages root development in these areas and the tree takes up the nutrients. This principle of encouraging root development in limited feeding areas is applied when the concentrate fertiliser sticks are used. The sticks are driven into the soil around the branch spread; this encourages root development and the tree takes up the determined amount of nutrients. Although the initial expense of the sticks may be higher than that of conventional fertilisers, considerable time is saved in application and it is likely that a greater percentage of the fertiliser would be used by the tree.

LIQUID FERTILISERS There are two methods of applying these. Compost drainage or concentrate liquids applied through a diluting machine are watered directly to the root feeding area. This area may need to be forked over and the liquid applied slowly to allow penetration before surface run-off away from the tree roots.

The second method is to apply liquids in the form of proprietary brand foliar feed. Application rates depend on the type of tree and in particular on type and size of leaf. There is a very efficient nutrient uptake through the leaf cuticle if the tree is in the right condition. The liquid is best applied through a knapsack mechanical sprayer under cloudy, warm, humid but dry conditions. This method of applying nutrients has obvious advantages if the root system is covered with concrete or a similar substance, but the nutrients are very quickly absorbed by the tree and are very short-lived. The major disadvantage is that the spraying of leaves of large mature trees, particularly in urban areas, is not really practicable.

As realisation of the need for tree feeding grows, other means of application should develop. Trunk injections, now a reality for tree pest and disease control, could be adapted for the application of nutrients. Pneumatic pressure guns are also utilised in the USA for forcing and distributing compound nutrients into the soil. If compressors are to be used by tree units for power-cutting equipment, a soil injection attachment could easily be fitted.

Seasons for application

It is essential to apply the nutrients when the tree can best utilise them. This means that the tree must be in an active state, otherwise the nutrients may well be leached from the soil before the tree can absorb them and benefit from the application. BULKY ORGANIC MATERIALS With their broader benefits of soil amelioration, these can be applied at most times of the year as long as the soil is not frozen or waterlogged.

SLOW-RELEASE COMPOUND CONCENTRATE FERTILISERS These are normally applied in spring or early summer to coincide with active tree growth. Autumn applications can induce late growth which may be vulnerable to frost damage. QUICK-ACTING TYPES Normally applied during the growing season.

10 Tree Felling and Disposal

Trees, like all life forms, have a natural limited life cycle. Tree life cycles can vary from tens and hundreds to even a thousand years and at any time during that period the tree may have to be felled for one or more of the following reasons.

Reasons for Felling

Safety

As has been mentioned in earlier chapters, trees can be weakened or killed by pests, diseases, animals, adverse weather conditions, the effects of man and natural senility. Regular inspections will note these weaknesses and a decision must be taken on the trees' safety related to surrounding hazards. If the trees are in a public place and there is a risk of personal injury or damage to property, then felling may well be the only safe course of action. Inexperienced people may well panic and remove trees that could be repaired, but even that is better than leaving obviously dangerous trees in public areas.

Hygiene

Many infectious pests and diseases may use comparatively healthy trees as a host during all or part of their life cycle. The only practical control may be to fell and burn the host tree.

Clearance

The reason for tree preservation orders is to prevent the unwarranted removal or mutilation of important trees. Many trees, however, are not that important or have such a limited safe life cycle that they ought to be cleared before any area is re-developed. When important trees are retained, due consideration should be given to the occupiers or users of the area as they can cause an intolerable nuisance. Better to fell trees when the area is clear and open than to have to fell, in sections, when building or other constructions are under or near the tree.

Laws that control felling are dealt with in Chapter 2.

Timber

One of the basic differences between arboriculture and forestry is that in arboriculture timber value is not normally the major reason for felling, and may not be considered at all. In fact, many of the trees used for arboricultural practices have little or no timber value owing to their species, their

shape, the state of the timber in the tree or the access to the tree. This does not mean that the tree surgeon cannot utilise or market the timber if it is of value. With the ever-increasing costs and value of timber its market potential should always be considered, if only for fuel or its chippings as mulch.

Thinning of woodlands is a sound practice for removing unwanted, dangerous or marketable trees and to allow for replacements. The objective and priorities of the woodland must be determined as old dying trees or even fallen trees may be of importance for conservation.

Methods of Felling

Once it has been agreed that a tree or a number of trees are to be felled, the method will depend on the proximity of surrounding features, the access for large machinery, whether or not the stump or roots are to be removed and the timber value. Tree felling is an operation beset with dangers and only skilled, properly equipped operators should attempt the work or supervise trainees.

Felling on open sites

Method 1: Bulldozer

On large, open development sites trees are often cleared in advance of building works. Little regard is given to timber value and large track-laying bulldozers are used first to cut the main anchor roots and then to push the whole tree over. Once on the ground, the trunk is cut with a chain saw and the tree is pushed on to the fire. With a good operator this operation can be very efficient and the whole tree, including roots and stump, is removed. However, this effective method has little regard for the timber of the tree, and if a valuable stick is to be felled, perhaps other methods should be adopted.

Method 2: Winches

Tractor or lorry-mounted power winches or hand winches can be used for pulling over even large trees. If the stump is also to be removed, the main support roots are first severed either by mechanical means or by hand grubbing. The steel wire winch rope should be attached as high as possible but still on strong enough wood to take the pull without breaking. The height gives leverage and the whole tree and stump can be pulled over.

Fig 30 Tree felling with chain saw
   Sink cut (left) removed and back cut parallel
   to it
→ Direction fall aided by wedge
   Tree falling with hinge, sink wide enough not
   to close before tree is nearly down
   Felling leaning tree by cutting from the hinge
   to the back

Winches are potentially very dangerous tools and only experienced operators should use them (see Chapter 4). Once down, the tree can be cut up and the wood and stump removed.

Method 3: Chain saws

Where trees are to be felled to ground level and the stump left or removed by alternative means the chain saw method is the most commonly used.

On open sites it is normal to fell the tree with its natural directional fall or, if necessary, to fell in the direction that will ease removal. Once the

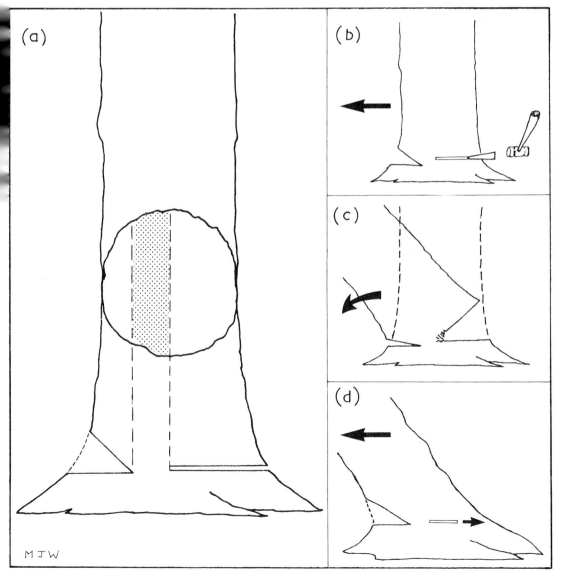

direction has been determined, the tree is prepared for felling. The first operation is to cut a directional wedge from the tree. When cutting this wedge or sink it is particularly important to ensure that it is in line with the intended fall. This requires practice, and if the first attempt is not correct it is better to start again, slightly higher.

If the tree has large buttress roots these may have to be removed before cutting out the sink. Once the sink has been removed the tree is severed through from the back towards the sink (fig 30). Again, this back cut must be accurate and must finish parallel to and not lower than the back of the sink. Depending on the natural weight of the tree, it may be necessary to pull the tree with a rope or winch in the direction of intended fall or to use felling wedges which are driven in behind the back cut. These wedges should be made of magnesium alloy or plastic so that they will not damage the chain saw.

The tree should fall with the hinge left between the back of the sink and the back cut.

When felling, the operator should check for dead or hanging branches which can fall when the tree starts to go over, and a clear escape route should be available if felling amongst undergrowth or other debris.

Many trees will present other problems and alternative methods may have to be practised. LEANING TREES should not be cut from the back as already described since the great tension will split the trunk as soon as it is severed. One method used for felling leaning trees is to remove the sink as before in line with the lean and then, rather than cutting towards the sink from the back, the chain saw is bored in behind the sink, leaving a hinge and cutting out towards the back of the tree (fig 30d).

BASAL ROTS are also a problem, and if the heartwood is rotten or weakened the hinge cannot be relied upon to hold the tree on the intended directional fall. If rots are noticed when cutting the sink, it may be safer to stop and cut the sink higher up the trunk above the basal rot. Experienced operators may be able to fell accurately even when the base is rotten or hollow, but if there is any doubt, the weight of the tree should first be removed by cutting off the main branch system.

SUSPENDED TREES that have blown over or have been felled and are lodged against other trees or structures present additional problems. Small trees can be rolled out by hand or with a winch whilst larger trees may have to be taken down in sections from the top. Great care should be taken when cutting the supporting wood and heavy equipment such as power winches or cranes may have to be used.

Felling on restricted sites

Felling on restricted sites will present other problems and alternative methods may have to be adopted. If the only restriction is access for large machinery, the trees can be felled by hand winches or chain saws as already described. But often there is not sufficient clearance to drop the tree in one then either the surrounding hazard is removed or the tree is felled away from the obstacles or in sections.

Method 1: Limited directional felling

When the obstacle is only on one side of the tree or if there is access to fell the tree in a limited direction, the tree can be felled as before in that direction. If the tree's natural weight is opposed to this direction, the branches on the heavy side are first removed to aid the fall of the tree in the required direction. If the whole tree is leaning against the required fall it may be very difficult to pull the tree against this lean, and felling in sections may be the only safe practice.

Method 2: Felling in sections

It is quite common to find trees, particularly in urban areas, completely surrounded by buildings, roads, fences, power and telephone lines and other hazards. If these trees have to be felled, the only way is to take the tree down in small sections and drop or lower the branches and trunk to the ground clear of the obstructions. This can be a very time-consuming operation, perhaps requiring special equipment and highly skilled staff. It is, therefore, often very expensive.

Frequently, owing to the lack of heavy machinery, or lack of access for it, this operation is carried out by a climber with chain saws. The top and side branches are removed first and dropped or lowered to the ground, depending on the proximity of surrounding features. During this initial work the climber will wear a normal tree-climbing safety harness. Once all the top and side branches have been removed, it remains to take down the main trunk. As there is no anchor point above the working position, the climber should use a pole belt and climbing irons (illustration 3 on page 25).

There are two main methods of taking down the trunk if it cannot be felled in one from ground level. The first method is to cut off small sections of trunk and push these off so that they fall to the base of the tree. A stack of brushwood at the base will help hold the sections in place when they fall. The climber works down the trunk cutting section after section. On large trees where heavy chain saws have to be used at height, this can be an arduous job and the second method can be employed.

Fig 31   Removing section of trunk with ropes
a   Sink removed first in direction of pull
b   Anchor rope in place
c   Section prepared for back cut
    (i) Pull-off rope
    (ii) Direction of back cut

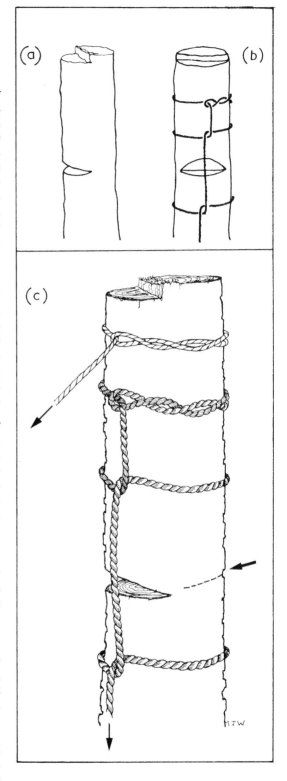

The second method is to take down larger sections of trunk by roping the cut section to a point below the cut. This operation is often called 'snatching'. The first part of this operation is to remove a sink, as in tree felling, at a determined distance from the top. A rope of adequate size is pulled up by the climber and attached below the sink, then pulled up in front of the sink and attached above it. The base of the rope is secured properly by the ground man. Once the main rope is in place a second pull-off rope is attached as high as possible on the section to be removed. The climber then cuts through from the back towards the sink. A hinge – of adequate thickness to hold before pulling – is left between the sink and the back-cut and the climber descends. By pulling on the pull-off rope the hinge can be broken and the section of trunk will topple over, being held by the anchor rope until lowered. On very smooth-barked trees it will be impossible to hold the cut section, but it will fall more slowly and close into the trunk (fig 31). This operation can then be repeated until the whole trunk is down.

Where there is access for machinery, much of the heavy, dangerous handwork can be avoided. Cranes of any size and reach can be employed to take the branches or trunks up and away after cutting, and hydraulic platforms can be used to put the operator in a safe, accessible situation where he can use ropes and saws without climbing.

Disposal of Wood

As mentioned earlier, all commercial outlets for wood should be explored, but often sales are limited or the effort not justified. There are various means of disposal.

Burning

In unrestricted sites burning can be a very effective means of disposal of all parts of the tree. Fires should be lit only with the owner's consent and should be carefully controlled and supervised.

Brushwood chippers

Where operators have a brushwood and cord wood disposal problem and burning is not permitted, brushwood cutters can be a very attractive alternative. The cost of buying or hiring such a machine must be compared with other disposal methods. Large machines can take up to 200mm (8in) cord wood and reduce the volume to one fifteenth of its former bulk.

Clearance from site

If burning is not permitted and brushwood chippers are not available or not practicable, the brushwood, cord wood and main trunk may have to be transported from the felling site and disposed of by tipping or burning elsewhere. Many councils prohibit tipping of brushwood and this situation can only deteriorate; therefore, other outlets may have to be sought. Small mechanical cranes can be used for lifting brush and cord wood such as Hyab cranes fitted on the back of a lorry. If staff have to lift wood they should be properly trained in the correct lifting methods.

If brushwood and cord wood are to be transported on the highway the load should be properly stacked and tied down.

Disposal of Stumps

The tree stump can be pulled out when felling as already mentioned. If the wood can be burnt on site there is only the problem of moving the stump to the fire. If a large stump has to be removed from site, heavy lifting equipment will have to be employed as it is difficult to cut the stump into small sections for manhandling. Stumps can also be buried on site but, again, large digging equipment will be required.

If the tree has been felled to ground level and the stump left, there are various means of disposing of or killing the stump.

Blasting

On open sites stumps can be blown out of the ground with explosives and the smaller pieces can be manhandled. A licence must be obtained from the local authority for the purchasing and storage and staff should be thoroughly trained in the proper storage, handling and use of explosives. Few local authorities would attempt this work and specialist contractors can be employed.

Hand grubbing and winching

Although laborious and time-consuming, the removal of stumps by hand grubbing and hand or mechanical winching is very frequently practised, owing to the unavailability of machinery or the limitations of other methods.

A trench should be cut some distance from the cut stump so that all main anchor roots can be severed. The winch rope can be attached to the side opposite from the pull and the stump pulled out of the hole. Care should be taken to ensure that the stump cannot fall or roll back into the

hole, particularly if the site is left unsupervised. The stump still has to be disposed of. Little or no access is required. Timber jacks can also be used.

Hydraulic lifting machines

A number of existing tractor-mounted machines can be used for aiding stump removal. A fore-end loader can cut away the soil to expose roots and a specially designed hydraulic lifting machine has been manufactured to fit on the back of the tractor. This 'Stumpmaster' can lift tree stumps up to 375mm (15in) trunk diameter. Once the stump is out of the ground the same machine can transport it on to a lorry or to the disposal area. Access for the tractor and machine is required.

Stump-cutting machines

If there is access for these machines, they are probably the most efficient means of dealing with stumps. The stump is quickly reduced to chips which can easily be disposed of. Whether such machines are purchased or hired will depend on the scale of the department or unit and the number of stumps to be removed.

Burning

Burning stumps *in situ* is effective but takes time and can cause considerable nuisance. Saltpetre and paraffin are poured into slits or holes in the stump surface and, once soaked in, ignited. Great care should be taken on peaty soils.

Stump-killing

If stumps are to be left, one problem can be the regrowth from the cut stump and from root suckers. This regrowth can be effectively killed by the application of total weedkillers. Two commonly used chemicals are ammonium sulphamate and sodium chlorate. (Details of these chemicals are given in Chapter 5, 'Materials and Chemicals'.) Both are highly soluble total weedkillers and are applied to the conductive tissues of the cut stump. Holes or slits can be drilled or cut 75–100mm (3–4in) into the stump and the chemical inserted. On older stumps these holes may need to be deeper or a frill girdle may have to be cut round the stump.

Care should be taken to avoid spillage of the chemical on to surrounding soil or plants. It may be necessary to cap the holes after filling to avoid run-off. The chemicals are translocated through to all parts of the stump and root system.

If neighbouring trees are in close proximity, there may be a risk of the toxic chemicals being transferred by root grafts. If this risk is apparent a trench should be cut between the killed stump and the neighbouring trees.

11 Contract Surgery

Once it has been determined what work is to be carried out, it is necessary to organise the work programme. Many local authorities and large estates have their own direct labour units and all or part of the tree work can be carried out under the direction and control of the responsible officer or agent. The great majority of tree owners, however, do not have staff or equipment, and tree work contractors are employed.

Employing Contractors

When contractors are to be employed it is advisable to check their standards of work and insurance and to indicate clearly what work is to be done by the preparation of a detailed specification.

Standards of work

Most tree work is irreversible, and untrained or inexperienced operators may not only disfigure or mutilate trees but also create dangers to life and property. The Arboricultural Association (incorporating the Association of British Tree Surgeons and Arborists) maintains a list of approved contractors. To qualify for inclusion on this list, contractors must work to BS3998, *Recommendations for Tree Work* (1966). Other companies can work to equally high standards, and here personal knowledge or recommendation is the best means of ascertaining the quality of their work. Reputable firms will always confirm quotations and present invoices on headed paper.

Insurance

It is essential that all companies carrying out tree work activities have adequate insurance coverage. Most important for the client and public is public liability coverage. It is a condition that all approved contractors on the Arboricultural Association's list must have a minimum of £250,000 public liability insurance coverage. It is advisable to check contractors' insurance documents before employing. Contractors should also have insurance coverage for their employees and vehicle insurance in accordance with the provisions of the Road Traffic Acts.

Specifications

Agreement must be established between the client and contractor for work to be done. For minor works verbal agreements are normally reached on site and these are confirmed by the contractor in writing before work commences. For larger scale operations it is advisable for the client to prepare a written specification detailing all works to be done and any conditions that must be adhered to. Such specifications should be prepared by experienced staff. If the client or owner does not have this knowledge, independent consultants can be employed to prepare the specification and arrange the contract. The Arboricultural Association also issues a Register of Arboricultural Consultants. Many employers of tree work contractors such as local authorities, state corporations and large firms of developers, architects and landscape architects will prepare their own specification and contract documents and invite competitive tenders for the work to be done.

The specification and contract documents are normally in three parts.

Part 1: Form of tender

The form of tender is the more formal part of the document which the contractor signs to confirm that he has examined the specification and work to be done and agrees to carry out the work as specified for a said sum. The form of tender also states the date by which the tender price must be submitted and any other clauses that the client may wish to include, eg reference to the Fair Wages Resolution, insurance coverage, commencement and completion dates, any provisional or contingency sums to be added to the tender price and conditions of payment. Many large authorities and firms have a standard list of such clauses which form part of any contract.

Part 2: Specification

This section sets out the general tree work clauses and specifies all the terms and operations included in the third part of the document, the schedule of work to be done on each tree. This specification should not tell the contractor how to do his job but should clearly state, without any ambiguity, what the job is and how it is to be carried out.

The general tree work preliminaries may specify any or all of the following, or others if necessary.
(i) SITE VISIT The contractor shall visit the site and make himself acquainted with the means of ingress and egress and site conditions, and will be deemed to have done so before tendering.
(ii) RESTRICTED SITE If any of the work necessitates the entrance to adjoining land the

contractor will make the necessary arrangements for access. The contractor shall not permit any of his workmen to wander about the area or to trespass on adjoining property.

(iii) SITE SUPERVISION The contractor will allow for adequate site supervision to guarantee standards of work and to safeguard public and property.

(iv) DAMAGE TO SITE The contractor will take care to avoid damaging any structures, fittings or neighbouring trees, shrubs, grass or surfaces and if any are damaged will undertake to reinstate or compensate to the satisfaction of the client.

(v) TRAFFIC AND PEDESTRIAN CONTROL AND WARNING The contractor will provide adequate warning signs and staff to ensure the safety of public and traffic during operations. Traffic warning signs should comply with Ministry of Transport Regulations, 1972.

(vi) SURROUNDING HAZARDS The contractor will take any surrounding hazards into consideration when submitting the tender and shall be responsible for any costs incurred in the disconnection and re-connection of overhead power lines and telephone cables or underground services. He shall also be responsible for arranging with the authorities concerned for the working and safety of such apparatus.

(vii) WORKMANSHIP The contractor shall employ only competent staff and the client reserves the right, at his discretion, to dismiss from the site any workman employed by the contractor.

(viii) SUB-CONTRACTORS Sub-contractors shall be allowed only with the prior consent of the client. The main contractor will ensure that any sub-contractor complies with the conditions of contract and specification.

(ix) DISPOSAL OF WOOD Brushwood and cord wood may/may not be burnt on site; or Brushwood and cord wood to be removed from site. Brushwood chippers are permitted so long as they do not cause a noise nuisance. All timber to be removed from site and credit for timber allowed for in the tender. All stumps to be removed from site; or Stump-cutting machine can be used.

(x) FIRES Fires may be made only with the prior consent of the client in the positions agreed. The contractor will accept all risks from such fires and will ensure that the public are properly safeguarded and that the ground is reinstated on completion; or No fires are allowed on site.

(xi) EXPLOSIVES The use of explosives will not be permitted except in certain circumstances and after agreement with the client. The contractor will accept all risks from such explosives and safeguard the public and property; or No explosives are allowed.

(xii) SAFETY STANDARDS All work is to be undertaken in strict accord with the general safety factors laid down in BS3998 (1966).

(xiii) NOTIFICATION The contractor shall notify the client before work is to commence and when the work is completed.

(xiv) SEASONS All work to be done at the appropriate season; see BS3998 (1966).

The actual tree work specification may include any or all of the following, depending on the work listed in the schedule.

(i) EQUIPMENT All plant and equipment should be appropriate for the task and in well maintained order. Tools to be surface sterilised after use on trees which are known or suspected to be diseased.

(ii) TREATMENT OF CUTS All final cuts to be made into living wood flush to its source. All cut surfaces over 50mm (2in) in dia to be treated as soon as possible or within the same day with an approved wound sealant (*specify actual type or types permitted*).

(iii) PRUNING OPERATIONS All pruning operations to take into account the natural appearance of the tree and public safety. (*Specify actual pruning operation, ie lifting of crown, cleaning out, crown thinning, reducing and shaping or crown renewal.*)

(iv) BARK WOUNDS All bark wounds to be cut back to sound undamaged wood, shaped to induce callus formation and treated with a tree paint (see clause (ii), Treatment of cuts).

(v) CAVITY WORK All cavities or rots to be opened and inspected and a report made to the client on the extent of the rot and the recommended treatment required. If the tree is to be retained, all rotten wood is to be removed back to sound wood which is then to be treated with a tree paint and/or wood preservative. (*Specify actual treatments, eg small shallow cavities, large deep cavities, water pockets.*)

(vi) BRACING (*Specify all material to be used, eg types and sizes of cables, screw eyes or eye bolts, positions, tension.*)

(vii) FEEDING (*Specify types of materials to be used, methods and rates of application.*)

(viii) FELLING (*Specify whether tree stump is to be removed or felled to ground level. If to ground level, define ground level, ie 25–50mm (1–2in) from soil level. If stump removed, specify depth and width of extraction.*)

(ix) ANCHORAGE No existing trees to be used as winch anchors without the prior consent of the client and adequate protection attached to the trees. (*Specify method of protection, or refer to BS3998.*)

(x) CLEARANCE OF SITE Contractor to leave the site clean and tidy and all wood, equipment and other materials to be removed to the satisfaction of the client.

Part 3: Schedule of work to be done

This section specifically tells the contractor what work is to be done on each tree.

On large-scale sites with several trees the schedule should be accompanied by a site plan with each tree numbered and the corresponding number attached to or painted on the tree. There is often a considerable timelag between tendering and commencing the work, so the client must ensure that the numbers are still legible and if, in fact, any variations should be allowed for in the schedule, eg trees could have died or have been blown over since the preparation of the specification.

The schedule is normally set out in table form with the tree number, species, work required to be done, and a column left for the contractor to insert his estimate of time and equipment required (Table 8).

Table 8: Typical schedule of work to be done

Tree no	Species	Work to be done	Estimate
1	Quercus robur	Thin crown by one-third Treat bark wound, north side of trunk at 1m	
2	Acer pseudoplatanus	Fell to ground level	
3	Acer pseudoplatanus	Fell to ground level	
4	Cedrus alantica	Clean out dead wood Support two horizontal branches with 9mm round strand cable	
5	Ulmus procera	Fell and remove stump and root system (0.5m deep, 2m diameter)	
6	Aesculus hippocastanum	Lift crown to 4m on all sides Inspect and report on cavity 5m on south side	

TOTAL: £

less credit for timber @ £

= £

plus contingencies/and/or provisional sum of £

Final TOTAL transferred to Form of Tender: £

Supervision of contract

It is important that all tree work contracts should be adequately supervised to ensure that the work is done in accordance with the specification. Reputable firms will not attempt to take short cuts, but it is only fair to the contractors who were not awarded the contract to make regular site visits to enforce the conditions of the specification.

Estimating and Costing

Most tree-surgery operations are labour-intensive and the estimate is normally based on the time taken to do the required work, depending on the method and equipment employed.

Man-day units

This time estimate is expressed as a unit and each unit normally represents one man for one day. Therefore, a nine-unit estimate will represent one man for nine days or three men for three days. Estimating is *not* guessing and only experienced staff can accurately forecast the amount of time required, taking into account the operation required and method, any surrounding hazards, the tools and equipment available and the efficiency of the tree work team.

Unit costs

Once the man-day units have been established, it is necessary to put a monetary value to each unit. This unit cost or charge must be arrived at accurately and the following must be taken into account.

LABOUR Including managerial, supervisory and operatives, clerical and additional professional staff including accountants, solicitors, etc.

TRANSPORT Including work vans or trucks, lorries, cars, tractors, etc; also capital costs, depreciation, running costs.

EQUIPMENT Including standard climbers' equipment, hand and mechanical tools, traffic warning signs, etc. Ropes. Bracing equipment, etc.

MATERIALS Including tree paints. Cavity fillers, etc. First aid materials.

DEPOT Including office accommodation and equipment, telephones, filing and accounts, stationery. Stores for materials and equipment and workshop. Garages for vehicles. Costs include rates, rents, maintenance, heating, lighting and cleaning.

INSURANCE Including public liability and employer liability and insurance of premises and vehicles.

ADVERTISING Including local and national press, professional journals, etc, exhibits at shows, etc.

PLUS ANY OTHER COSTS Including taxation and profit.

Many of the costs will vary and it is important to re-assess actual costs frequently. Once the total costs are established this amount must be recouped by the unit cost, including the profit margin. Thus the actual amount estimated for any job is the number of units multiplied by the cost per unit plus any extra cost such as hire of special equipment, charges for dismantling power cables, etc.

Bonus Schemes

Few tree-surgery operations are repetitive enough to establish any timed or measured incentive bonus scheme, but if a tree work team is working to an estimated time unit for any job it is possible to pay a bonus on any time saved. For example: estimated time – nine units; actual time taken – eight units; therefore, a saving of one unit and staff could be paid a percentage of that time saved. There is always the risk that staff may be tempted to lower standards of work or safety standards to achieve their bonus, and any scheme devised must be well supervised with regular checks on safety and work standards.

It is important that land owners know what trees they have on their land and have a reasonable knowledge of their condition. A tree survey can establish where the trees are situated, their proximity to surrounding features, their type, dimensions, age, condition and amenity value. A more detailed inspection may be required to repair the trees or safeguard public and property.

Tree Surveys

Objectives

The objectives of and reasons for the survey must be clearly established and the survey carried out to meet these requirements. Local authorities carry out detailed surveys of trees on council property, particularly those growing on highways, at school sites, in parks, etc, to plan a work programme of maintenance and replacements.

If a site is to be developed, it is important to carry out a tree survey to plot and safeguard trees of important amenity value.

Surveys may be carried out over large-scale areas to establish the overall tree cover, hedgerows, woodlands or presence of pathogens. It may well be impractical to carry out large-scale surveys completely or on foot and sample surveys or aerial photography may be used.

Methods

Once the objectives of the survey are known the details to be recorded and the method must be decided.

1 Towns A tree survey of a town or district is normally carried out to determine what trees are present. Such a survey needs careful planning and co-ordination between the departments of the authority. The area can easily be divided into parks, open spaces, school sites, cemeteries, highways, etc, and each section can be surveyed independently, building up to a complete record of the whole area.

A large open space such as a park or school ground is normally accompanied by a scale drawing where all the trees can be accurately located and numbered, and a schedule or recording form is designed and used to enter the detail required. Information usually recorded is: tree number, species, dimensions, age, condition, and planting and maintenance records. Once recorded, this information can be updated as trees are removed or replaced and can form the basis of a regular, more detailed tree inspection programme.

When planning a highway or street tree survey, a town map is used as a basis for the survey, and rather than a scale plan and numbering system, the trees can be recorded by road name and house number. Such a survey should record the tree species, dimensions, condition and planting and maintenance records as before and also such other detail as proximity to surrounding features and hazards. As street trees normally require regular maintenance, removal and replanting, the information recorded is perhaps best transferred to a card index system, filed under street names and house numbers. As the trees are maintained or removed the cards can be amended and additional cards can be added when new trees are planted.

2 Development sites If trees are to be successfully retained on a development site it is essential to carry out a detailed tree survey to determine which trees are of important amenity value and to take effective steps to protect them (see Chapter 13). The tree survey should be carried out before the planning of the new development, then if trees are of real importance due consideration can be given to them by siting the constructions, roads, building works, etc well clear of the trees. Unimportant or dangerous trees can be removed before site work commences.

Site plan

A scale plan is normally required which should accurately locate all existing features, such as buildings, roads, ditches, trees, hedges and contour levels. The scale of the plan should be large enough for all trees to be clearly identified. 1/500 scale is particularly useful, though 1/1250 scale will cover a larger area and still be large enough to locate individual trees. On very large sites it may be necessary to divide the plan into sections. It is of particular importance that the tree trunks are accurately plotted on the plan.

Numbering trees

The tree positions on the plan can be numbered in a logical sequence so that each tree can be surveyed and the information recorded. The trees on site can then be numbered to correspond with the plan. There are several methods of numbering and the ideal type would give clarity, durability and removability.

The numbers can be painted on the trunks. This is satisfactory only if the paint lasts long enough for the full site work to be completed and is not too durable to leave unsightly numbers on the tree long after the development has been completed.

Small numbered metal tags are particularly useful as they are very durable and can be removed when the site has been completed. They are, however, easily removed by vandals. If used they are best tacked on to the trunk at a regular height and position so that no time is wasted looking for the tag if it is missing.

Information required

The information required in each tree survey must be established and this may vary depending on circumstances. The following information is normally required.

TREE SPECIES   The botanical name is preferable to common English names as it is more exact and free from ambiguities. It is important to identify the tree, as species react differently to site work and their normal life expectancy and size may be of importance when deciding whether to retain them.

DIMENSIONS   The tree's size is of particular importance and some care and accuracy is necessary to establish the following dimensions:

1   Height from ground level to top branch. This can be accurately measured by a pocket hypsometer or clinometer.

2   Clear trunk measured from ground level to first branches at trunk or ground clearance at branch spread.

3   Trunk diameter measured with calipers or a diameter tape which is placed round the circumference and reads off in diameters. This measurement is normally taken at standard breast height – 1·3m (4ft 3in).

4   Crown spread is all too often just measured from one side of the branch spread to the other and assumes that the trunk is in the centre. A more accurate and detailed crown spread survey would measure the spread of the branches from the trunk to the points of the compass. Where trees are growing in groups or in rows where the crown spreads unite, the survey can measure the extreme spreads of the group related to the tree number.

AGE OF TREE   It may be difficult or impossible to state the age of the tree accurately. Young, semi-mature, mature and over-mature are age categories that will normally suffice. Life expectancy may be of more relevance, and this can be judged only by knowing the species and the existing and future conditions and treatments of the tree and its surrounds.

CONDITION OF TREE   The survey can record the overall condition of the tree, eg healthy, crown die-back, dead, requires tree surgery or requires

more detailed climbing inspection or test boring.

SURROUNDING   FEATURES   Any surrounding features that may have a bearing on the tree should be recorded, eg overhead power and telephone lines, ditches, buildings.

AMENITY VALUE   Based on the tree species, size, age, condition and situation, the trees can be categorised in various groups and each group can be represented by a code symbol. Several systems of coding are used and so long as all concerned with the planning of the development and protection of the trees are fully conversant with the code, there is room for flexibility. An example of a code is as follows:

A   Important trees, save at all costs

B   Sound trees of less importance than 'A' trees

C   Suspect trees, require further inspection or treatment before final categorising

D   Dead, dangerous trees or trees of little consequence on the site

E   Transplantable trees

A colour code can be linked to the letter code and the trees on the site plan coloured according to their value to give an overall picture of the trees on the site. If a monetary value is to be established, the code can be linked to valuation systems.

Recording information

Some form of tree survey schedule is required to record the information. The schedule should be designed to cover all factors (Table 9). The schedule is taken on site and all information recorded. Site conditions are often difficult and a large site plan, schedule and measuring equipment can prove cumbersome. One way of easing this is to use a pocket tape recorder so that the information can be transcribed in more favourable surroundings.

Use of survey information

Once the survey is finished and the site plan completed with crown spreads and colour code, the important trees can be noted and then the development planned – avoiding important trees if possible. Unwanted trees can be removed and retained trees protected before site work commences.

3   Large-scale surveys   When large-scale surveys, covering perhaps complete areas, counties or regions, are carried out, detailed tree surveys are not practicable and are not necessarily required. Sample surveys can be used to build up an

Table 9: Tree Survey Schedule

SITE .... PLAN REF NO .... SURVEYED BY .... DATE............................

SHEET NO ....

Tree no	Species	Height	Clear trunk	Trunk dia	Crown spreads	Age	Condition	Surrounding features	Code
1	Quercus robur	23m	5m	1.4m	From trunk N– 7m W– 9m S–12m E– 5m	Mature	Sound, healthy, requires cleaning out	House 10m to north Hard surface 5m to south	A
2	Fraxinus excelsior	19m	3m	0.7m	N– 3m W– 5m SW– 6m S– 5m E– 4m	Mature	Signs of cavities and crown die-back, requires inspection	Open ground	C
3	Acer platanoides			0.5m	N– 3m				
4	,,			0.3m	E– 3m				
5	,,	16–18m	2–3m	0.4m	W– 4m	Semi-mature	Site boundary trees, important visual screen	Ditch 1m to west side Open ground to east Telephone line 2m to west	A
6	,,			0.5m	E– 5m				
7	,,			0.4m	S– 3m				

estimate of, say, diseased elm trees or the species of trees in an area. Aerial photography is a very useful method of surveying woodland areas to determine species, sizes, density, clearings, tracks, etc.

4 Statistical surveys A number of research programmes are being carried out to determine specific tree factors. A tree root survey is being carried out by the Royal Botanic Gardens, Kew. This is to determine the extent or spread and depth of tree roots. The information required has been reproduced on a survey card and when sufficient data have been collected the information can be computerised and valuable facts on root spreads and depths of a variety of tree species and soil types will be available.

The Arboricultural Association is carrying out a survey of uncommon and new trees. Members are asked to complete a form giving full details of trees. It is hoped to collect information on the performance of uncommon and new cultivars and some established varieties.

Tree Inspections

Trees, like all living organisms, are prone to attack and damage from a whole range of natural and unnatural agencies. Depending on the extent of the damage, the size of the tree and its proximity to surrounding features, the overall condition and safety of the tree must be determined. Tree inspections are, therefore, a very important aspect of tree maintenance and should be carried out only by experienced staff.

Objectives

The objective of a tree inspection is to establish the overall condition of the tree and to determine any remedial or removal action that may be required to safeguard the tree or, perhaps more important, the public or surrounding features.

Methods

Before carrying out an inspection the staff must be properly trained and equipped. The knowledge required can be built up only with training and experience. The inspector must know the normal characteristics of tree species, be able to recognise abnormalities and know the effects of any damage in both the short and long term. He will also need to know of remedial treatments and their effectiveness.

Detailed inspections of mature trees cannot always be completed by an external observation from ground level, although this can be assisted by binoculars. If structural weaknesses are observed from the ground, a climbing inspection may be necessary to determine the safety of the tree and the treatment required. Many weaknesses may be impossible to see from the ground, and large trees in public areas will require a climber's report.

If a number of trees are to be inspected the operation may need to be planned on the same lines as the tree survey, with a site plan, numbering and an information recording sheet. Where only one tree is to be inspected the observations and recommendations can be recorded on a tree report form.

43 Obvious danger symptom of crown die back
with weak, heavy branches over road

42 Detail of trunk showing fungal frúiting
bodies from faulty pruning stumps

Whatever the scale of the operation, each tree must be individually examined and recommendations for action decided.

The inspector must observe the overall condition of the tree, taking into account its species, age, size and surrounding features. He should note and consider any abnormality and danger symptoms. All parts of the tree are liable to damage and the inspection should cover the entire tree, as a disorder in one part could seriously affect another and the overall health and safety of the tree.

Danger symptoms

Leaves

The leaf, being one of the most temporary parts of the tree, will often show symptoms of disorders either by direct damage or by damage to the roots or conductive tissues. Anything other than the normal leaf size, shape and colour should be investigated and the cause determined before remedial treatment can be recommended. Early leaf fall or late flushing may well indicate trouble elsewhere in the tree. Even in the dormant season, the leaf buds will tell much the same story. Healthy buds suggest a good root system and conductive tissues.

Twigs

The even distribution and growth of annual shoot extension will again indicate the overall vigour and health of the tree. Poor shoot growth or twig die-back, particularly in the upper crown, indicates root or soil problems.

Branch system

Lower and central branches may well die by natural suppression by the upper canopy. If dead branches of any size are present they could be a direct hazard to people or property beneath or will give rise to the formation of rots and cavities in the main trunk system. Over-dense crowns could cause a nuisance to surrounding features and are far more liable to wind damage. Crossing branches may chafe and cause breakage. When trees squeak or creak in the wind it is usually only two branches rubbing together. Unbalanced crowns may or may not be dangerous depending on the support wood on the trunk and the proximity to surrounding features. The greatest danger is when a tree has grown to one side because of a neighbouring tree or structure, and that adjacent feature is removed leaving the tree exposed.

Trunk system

The trunk system supports the upper crown and conducts water and foodstuffs up and down the tree. If any part of the trunk is weakened or destroyed the tree will become dangerous or the leaves and roots will suffer.

Weak trunk or major branch formations, particularly tight-forked trunks, are potentially dangerous and their safety must be determined. Old branch stumps or previously cut surfaces should be carefully examined for any signs of rot and treated as necessary. Trees that have been previously lopped or pollarded are a particular problem, especially if there has been major regrowth from the original cuts. Any signs of cavities or dead or damaged bark should be investigated and treated. The woodpecker's hole is a clear indication of internal rot. Many of the major heart-wood rotting fungi produce their fructifications on the trunk or main branch system. If there is any sign of these brackets this will indicate internal rot. Test boring will be necessary to determine the extent of the rot.

The inspection should also note any unwanted items in the tree such as metal clamps, boards, nests, climbing plants. These can be removed if causing damage. Ivy itself is not particularly damaging on the trunk unless it becomes too dominant in the crown. The main problem may be that the ivy will cover and hide other defects such as cavities, weak branch formations, etc.

Base of the tree

The butt of the trunk is the vital support area of the whole tree and any damage or weakness here could result in the whole tree collapsing. There are a number of wood-rotting organisms that will cause internal basal or butt rots. These are so common that it is normal practice to test-bore the base of any large mature tree which is growing in a public place.

Test-boring is carried out to see if any rot exists and, if it does, its extent. Only then can the overall safety of the tree be determined. Hand and power augers, as used in cable bracing, are useful for boring. A 6mm or 9mm ($\frac{1}{4}$–$\frac{3}{8}$in) bit is normally used and its length should be sufficient to reach the centre of the trunk. An experienced inspector can tell by the effort required when drilling and by the sawdust just how healthy or sound the wood is. A Swedish Increment borer is very useful for trunk inspection as a core is removed from the heart-wood which can be carefully examined either in the field or in a laboratory.

If it is decided that the tree can be retained the test bore-hole should be plugged. If wooden dowels are used these must be treated with a wood preservative. PO Compound, as described in Chapter 9, is very useful for plugging.

Many open-grown trees will develop strong

buttress roots to help support the trunk. If sheltered trees are exposed, these may well not have developed this support wood and may, therefore, be potentially dangerous and liable to wind throw.

Root system

Although it is impossible to inspect the roots of a tree, the root growing area should be carefully examined. Common danger symptoms are as follows:

1   Signs of parasitic organisms such as the fruiting bodies of harmful fungi, particularly honey fungus. The honey-coloured clump of toadstools appear in the autumn. Further inspection, by lifting the bark of the buttress roots or base of the tree, may well confirm this widespread disease by the presence of distinctive black strands called rhyzomorphs. The fruiting bodies of the conifer butt rot, *Fomes annosus*, are often found in exposed root areas such as animal burrows.

2   Alteration to soil levels or surfaces, particularly on development sites, results in many tree deaths. The lowering of soil levels may well remove major portions of the fibrous root system or, if drastic, may affect the stability and safety of the tree. Trenches cut within the root-spread area will have the same effect. If levels are raised' with non-porous material the roots will be suffocated, or if raised around the trunk the bark will be killed. Changes of soil surfaces can be just as damaging by cutting off the roots' air and water supply, by solid covering or by compaction (see Chapter 13).

3   Flooding or drought conditions will have a serious effect on the delicate root hairs if they persist for more than a few days. If such conditions exist remedial action must be taken at once.

4   The presence of any toxic substances must be carefully examined; once they have been identified, an antidote must be applied.

Recommendations for action

Once the whole tree has been inspected and defects or danger symptoms noted a judgement must be made on the overall safety of the tree in relation to surrounding features. If it is decided that the tree is dangerous or potentially dangerous, no delay should occur before the tree is felled. When it is recommended that the tree can be repaired, the inspector must relate the fault to the appropriate treatment. The effectiveness of any treatment must be carefully studied and the tree must be regularly re-inspected.

Seasons and frequency of inspections

Trees will show different symptoms depending on the time of year, and it is therefore advisable to inspect large trees once during the active growing period and once in the dormant season.

Young or obviously healthy trees will perhaps need inspection only annually or even bi-annually. Trees that have known defects will require more frequent inspections, particularly if there is the presence of any rapidly spreading parasitic organisms.

Evidence of tree inspections and treatments may be important in the event of any person taking action against the owner for damage incurred by the tree or part of the tree falling.

13 Care of Trees on Development Sites

Despite greater public awareness of the value of the environment there still remains a great deal of misunderstanding, ignorance and apathy when existing trees are threatened by the development or re-development of an area. Proposed developments require outline planning permission from the local planning authority and if the site contains trees it is at this stage that arboricultural expertise should be employed.

Initially, the arboriculturist should familiarise himself with the site and the number and general condition of the trees. This brief initial survey should be related to the proposed development and, if it is feasible to retain the trees, the full powers and knowledge of the local planning authority and the arboriculturist should be employed to protect them effectively. If the trees are not of any great consequence or amenity value or if the development is of such density that it would be difficult to safeguard the trees adequately, it may be better to clear the area and spend any available money on a comprehensive planting programme.

Effects of Development on Trees

Before taking steps to protect trees intended for retention, it is necessary to appreciate the special problems created by developments. The following are the most common difficulties encountered, and their effects on a tree will depend greatly on its species, age and health and on the degree of disturbance.

Alteration to site levels

Probably the most common reason for injury or death of trees on development sites is damage to the root system. Many architects and developers either fail to realise that the trees have and need roots or they hide damage by backfill and hope that the effects will not be serious or noticed. The raising or lowering of site levels can seriously affect trees. The effects of such action will depend on the proximity of the tree.

Alterations within the crown spread

The removal of soil around the tree directly damages the feeding and/or anchor roots. The raising of levels under the tree canopy can be just as damaging with the effect of compacting the existing levels, preventing air reaching the roots, and altering the water table. The raising of levels around the trunk will have the effect of creating dark, damp conditions which could damage or kill the bark and the conductive tissues.

The amount of removal or raising of soil and the depths and tolerances of trees will vary but it is advised that the levels within the crown spread should not be altered. Fastigiate or ascending trees will need careful treatment as the root system will obviously spread much further than the crown.

Alteration of overall site levels

Obviously the proposed developments will necessitate alteration to site levels, and so long as these are outside the crown spread they should not have any immediate effect on the trees. The major effect in the long term is the alteration to overall water levels.

Deep foundations and trenches can lower the water table permanently and in dry seasons the trees may suffer if not irrigated. The creating of mounds or tipping of spoil or soil over a large area can have the opposite effect of raising the water table with serious long-term effects on mature trees. Such conditions must be noted and corrected by adequate drainage away from the tree roots.

Developments may well affect the existing drainage system of the area and great care and vigilance should be exercised to correct any drainage problems. Good developments should not create damp or flooded conditions, but surface water may be taken away through the sewerage system, resulting in very dry conditions.

Alterations to soil surfaces

The effect of altering the soil surface around the tree is to prevent the natural supply of water and nutrients to the roots. The problem, again, is mainly confined to the area of the root spread. If it is necessary to cover the soil area, only porous materials should be used. Surface water from paved areas should not be drained into tree areas as the water could contain toxic properties.

Effects of site works

There are many other site operations that can have a serious effect on the trees.

Temporary buildings

Most construction developments need an array of site huts for storage and messrooms. If left to their own initiative, the builders will often erect these huts under the shelter and shade of trees. This should be avoided for the following reasons.

1 The huts, if left for any period of time, will create very dry conditions beneath.

2 Many toxic substances may well be stored in or around the huts and spillage can often occur.

3 One person is normally allocated the job of tea-making and cleaning up and seems to enjoy a daily burn-up of old papers and any other unwanted combustible materials. Again, these small fires can have a very serious effect on the trees' roots, branches and trunks.

Storage areas

Apart from the small materials stored in or around the site huts, most developments require space for the storage of bulky top and sub-soil and building materials. As has already been mentioned, no storage of soil, aggregate or toxic materials should be permitted under the branch spread of a tree. Frequently there is very little space left for storage and it may be necessary to allow the builders to store certain non-toxic or damaging materials beneath the trees. Such items as window frames or timber should not have any serious effects on the trees.

Parking

The parking of vehicles beneath the trees must be avoided. The effects can be very damaging both by soil compaction and by the spillage of fuel and oil. Again, if left to their own resources the builders will utilise the shelter and shade afforded by the trees.

Access routes

Large-scale developments often require a regular supply of construction materials, and if compaction and rutting are to be avoided, all vehicles must be diverted clear of existing trees.

Fires

In both the demolition and the final clearing operations developers often remove vast quantities of combustible debris by burning. Strict control must be asserted to ensure that such fires are lit well clear of the trees. On peaty soils it may be advisable to ban any fire-lighting.

Cranes

Many new developments are constructed in sections with the aid of large tower cranes. The siting of these cranes is important to avoid damage to tree crowns when lifting the sections or concrete hoppers from the delivery site to the building.

Site clearance

Many urban renewal programmes necessitate the demolition of existing buildings and structures before the developments begin. There is great risk to trees here with heavy demolition plant and fires. Unwanted trees are best removed before the new developments commence and, again, great care must be exercised to avoid damage to trees earmarked for retention, both by the actual felling operations and by access for vehicles for extraction.

Use of herbicides

It is quite common for developers to use total persistent weedkillers to control weed growth, and care must be afforded to prevent this being sprayed beneath retained trees.

Effects of tall buildings on trees

The construction of high-rise buildings in close proximity to trees can create adverse weather conditions. The most serious problems are wind and the dry, draughty conditions associated with these buildings. If the trees were previously in a natural sheltered position the effect can be very serious. Little can be done to offset this little researched problem, but due consideration should be given to the retention of the trees when it is known that these conditions will exist.

Effects of Trees on Buildings

Although this chapter is concerned with the healthy retention and replacement of trees, it is necessary to be aware of the adverse effect of large and vigorous trees on buildings. The two main problems are the nuisance that trees can create if situated close to buildings and the structural damage that can be caused by vigorous trees, particularly on shrinkable clay soils.

Nuisance by trees

Trees can create many problems for occupiers and neighbours, and this is discussed more thoroughly in Chapter 2. On new developments it is advisable to consider the occupiers who, although they may appreciate the aesthetic qualities of the trees, have a right to reasonable living conditions. The common sources of complaint which could lead to the eventual removal of a tree are:

1 Shade problems – particularly with heavy leaved and evergreen trees which may block light from windows and gardens.

2 Leaf litter, which blocks gutters and drains.

3 Roosting birds, which have many aesthetic qualities but can cause considerable nuisance by their droppings and noise.

4 The tree's safety, which in extreme weather conditions can never be guaranteed. It is important to ensure that trees which are retained in close proximity to public areas are in a safe condition and are regularly re-inspected.

Structural damage by trees

There have been many cases of trees damaging structures, and this problem should be recognised and considered by the developers and arboricultural staff when deciding on tree retention and siting of structures.

This problem has long been recognised by the building industry, and in 1969 the National House Builders Registration Council issued its Practice Note No 3, *Root Damage by Trees – Siting of Dwellings and Special Precautions*. This leaflet, available from the NHBRC, 58 Portland Place, London W1N 4BU, gives guidance on safe distances at which houses, garages, drains, walls, etc can be constructed from existing trees. The recommendation applies to all trees including trees on adjoining sites, and the height of the tree refers to its ultimate height when fully grown. If the recommendations are not adhered to it is likely that the NHBRC's ten-year guarantee will not be issued.

Without special constructional precautions, the following minimum distances are recommended.
ON CLAY SOILS Poplars and willows – do not build within a radius equal to the height of the tree. Other species – do not build within two-thirds of the height of the tree.
ON ALL OTHER SOILS Site the dwellings so that there is no risk of roots pushing against foundations or gaining entry to drains, and so that no more than 25 per cent of the roots need to be removed. In no case should the dwellings be sited closer than 12ft or one-third of the height of the tree, whichever is the less.
GROUPS OF TREES All the above distances must be increased by 50 per cent where there are rows or groups of trees.

When constructional precautions are taken, it may be possible to build nearer to a tree, but builders should obtain agreement from the NHBRC.

If it is decided that it is not practicable to allow the specified distances or if special precautions are too expensive, the only alternative will be to fell the trees. The leaflet points out that if trees are removed, clay soils may swell and some precautions could still be necessary.

These recommendations seem fair and reasonable, and of course developers should always be encouraged to site dwellings well clear of trees both for structural and nuisance reasons and for the wellbeing of the trees.

Tree Protection

Once outline planning permission has been sought and it has been decided that existing trees are worthy of retention, the arboriculturist should start to take active steps to protect them. Effective protection should commence with a detailed tree survey to determine which trees are worthy of retention, and then all stages of the development should be followed, from planning and siting of structures to the final landscape treatments.

Detailed surveys

Tree surveys

A detailed tree survey should be carried out prior to the planning stage to determine which trees are of amenity value and are in good enough condition to warrant protection, which may be expensive. The methods of carrying out and recording surveys for trees on development sites are detailed in Chapter 12. Once the survey is completed, the arboriculturist can advise on the siting of the development to avoid important trees.

Basic site surveys

As well as the tree survey, the arboriculturist should familiarise himself with the more general factors of the site. Details should be recorded of the following.
CLIMATIC CONDITIONS This should include rainfall, prevailing wind, exposure, frost pockets etc, and any other factors such as sea winds and atmospheric pollution.
SOIL CONDITIONS The type and depth of soil and subsoil will have a very important bearing on the safe retention of trees. With heavy clay soils the problems of structural damage to buildings and soil compaction are major considerations, and with light, sandy, free-drained soils there is the very real risk of drought conditions if the original water table is altered by the development. There is also the added fire risk with peaty soils.
LAND FORM AND DRAINAGE The existing contours and drainage systems are of particular importance if levels or the water table are to be altered. Even on small sites it is unusual for levels not to be altered, and even minor changes of level can have a major effect on trees.

Site planning

Although there are many factors to be considered when siting structures on a new development, it is the arboriculturist's duty, armed with the detailed tree survey and knowledge of site conditions, to advise and safeguard the important trees. Many architects and developers are very tree-conscious and will listen to accurate information and take heed of informed opinion. As more senior arboricultural appointments are made, more local planning authorities will be able to call on this expertise.

The arboriculturist should advise on the amenity value and condition of individual trees and groups of trees and the effects on them of the proposed developments. On high-density developments, space will be at a premium and decisions must be taken as to whether or not a tree can effectively be retained with a useful life span, and without causing too much annoyance to the occupiers.

Site clearance

Once agreement has been reached, the arboriculturist will know which trees are to be removed and which retained. Unwanted trees are best removed before site works commence when there will be more space for felling and clearance. Care should be taken not to damage the retained trees. If demolition work is to be carried out, again great care and protection should be afforded the retained trees.

Protection of retained trees

All retained trees will need effective protection during all stages of site clearance, construction and final landscape treatments. The protection needs to be administered in various ways, and if the following measures are vigorously applied there is every chance of the trees remaining in good health.

Legal protection

On privately owned sites and, in some cases, local authority sites, the local planning authority has the power to protect the retained trees with tree preservation orders and to impose conditions within the planning permission. Recent legislation has improved the effectiveness of TPOs (see Chapter 2). It is difficult for the planning authority staff to determine what constitutes damage, particularly if no arboricultural advice is sought. A tree's roots may be severely damaged by any of the means mentioned earlier in the chapter, and the tree may survive for a few years. Although the tree eventually dies or has to be removed for safety's sake, no laws have been broken.

Where the development is on publicly owned land, TPOs are not normally applied, but it is important to safeguard the trees by stating clearly what must and must not be done in the building specification. Again, arboricultural expertise should be sought when preparing the specification.

Physical protection

Whatever legal protection is afforded, it is vital to erect strong physical barriers around the trees before any site works commence. As mentioned earlier, most of the damage will occur to the root system and it is important that the barrier should effectively protect the roots as well as the aerial parts of the tree. Barriers should, therefore, be positioned at least as far out as the branch spread on broad-crowned trees and the equivalent distance on ascending crown forms.

The barriers must be strong enough to withstand the stresses and strains of the development with heavy plant and materials perhaps on site for two or three years. A 2m-high scaffold pole barrier with chestnut fencing is usually strong and durable enough and can be re-used. Preserved wooden posts with corrugated iron sheeting can also be used successfully. The barriers can be erected around individual trees or around groups of trees or edges of woodlands.

The barrier will prevent the alteration of levels and surfaces, the parking of vehicles and the erection of site huts. It may be necessary to allow the storage of non-damaging materials inside the barriers, but this must be carefully controlled.

Communications

It is as well to enlist the co-operation of the site workers and, in particular, the clerk of works to keep a constant watch on the building work and the barriers. Many of these people just do not realise the damage they might cause and may well assist with the tree preservation policy if made aware of the tree's importance.

Site visits

Despite all the aforementioned safeguards, it is important that the arboricultural staff visit the site as frequently as possible to ensure that all is well. This may prove difficult where the arboriculturist covers a large area and has many sites under construction at the same time, thus emphasising the importance of good communications with the clerk of works. Any emergency tree work should be dealt with.

Final landscape treatments

When all the major constructions are nearing completion, the final landscape works usually commence. Landscape staff will normally have a good appreciation of tree care but this should not be taken for granted. Once the barriers are removed, the soil levels or surfaces may be altered and, since this is often carried out by mechanical means, it requires careful supervision by arboricultural staff.

However effective the protection has been, tree planting should be carried out to complement the existing trees and new structures and add continuity to the tree scene.

Remedial tree surgery

On completion of all works it will be necessary to inspect every tree and carry out any necessary remedial tree-surgery operations. The trees should be regularly inspected in the ensuing years to check for any deterioration and to maintain the newly planted trees.

Tolerances of Trees

The tolerance of trees to site works has never been thoroughly researched. The most serious problem is that of root damage and very little has been published on this particular point.

It is best to assume that no tree will tolerate a great degree of disturbance and obviously the older the tree, especially if suffering from any defect, the more liable it will be to injury or death from site disturbance. It has been found from experience, however, that certain trees are more liable to serious effects of damage than others.

Intolerant trees

The oak, even when still comparatively young, has proved to be very susceptible to die-back and death if the roots are disturbed and great care should be exercised when oaks are in the vicinity of site works. Although perhaps not as vulnerable as the oak, ash, birch, beech and most conifers should be given wide clearance and extra care.

Tolerant trees

Most trees when young will stand a fair degree of disturbance, and the following species have shown tolerance to root disturbance when in good health: planes, poplars, willows, thorns, and to some extent the redwoods, sequoia and sequoiadendron.

Before any conclusive lists can be prepared, a vast amount of data must be collated, ie investigated species, amount of disturbance, soil type and any other relevant information affecting site conditions.

Appendix:

Education and Training

A comprehensive and thorough education and training programme is not only an essential safety feature, but is also necessary to maintain and improve standards of work and to recruit the right calibre of new entrant by offering a rewarding career structure.

Tree surgery education and training can only be considered as part of the broader field of arboriculture, and arboricultural education has only comparatively recently been recognised as an entity in its own right.

Arboriculture has been part of the syllabus of horticultural and forestry courses for many years, as has the informal approach of on-the-job training, or working with and learning by the actions of others. This latter method is only as good as the skill of the operator and his ability to impart his knowledge.

Developments in Arboricultural Education and Training

The establishment, in the late fifties, of the Royal Forestry Society's Certificate and National Diploma in Arboriculture was the first major step in creating a recognised examination and career structure. These are examinations with no related courses and many students of horticulture and forestry and those working in the arboricultural industry are able to prove their knowledge by qualifying.

In the mid-sixties specialist arboricultural courses began to emerge. A number of day and evening classes were organised throughout the country, and a three-week course in preparation for the Certificate in Arboriculture was offered at the Cumberland and Westmorland College of Agriculture and Forestry (now Cumbria College), Newton Rigg, Penrith.

In 1968 the Association of British Tree Surgeons & Arborists approached Merrist Wood Agricultural College to provide a more comprehensive training programme in tree surgery. The ten-week Tree Surgery course for craftsmen and the three-week Tree Surgery course for foremen were established.

Two years later the Association, through its annual conference and in conjunction with the Arboricultural Association, promoted a Joint Working Party to study the needs and requirements of arboricultural education. This Joint Working Party was reconstituted as the Standing Committee on Arboricultural Education with representatives of most of the associations and bodies concerned with arboriculture and related subjects. The Standing Committee studies proposals and makes recommendations on arboricultural education to the appropriate government departments and committees.

Courses and Schemes Available

When considering or planning education or training programmes, it is necessary to decide carefully the objectives of the scheme, the needs of the industry and those of the individual. There is undoubtedly an ever-increasing demand for fully trained staff at various levels in both public and private sectors.

The four main levels or areas of work in arboriculture are Craftsman, Supervisor, Manager and Technologist. All require some form of education and/or training and the following schemes have been or are being developed at these levels. Selection or progression to any of these schemes depends on the individual's ability and ambition and on the job opportunities in the industry.

Craftsmen

Those employed in the public sector can enter the Local Government Training Board's New Entrant Training Scheme. This scheme with on-the-job practical training and off-the-job education has a category for arboriculture.

After the introductory training, new entrants can decide on an education course at a college and/or a practical modular programme. Progression through this scheme is linked to pay scales. Further details of the scheme are obtainable from the Local Government Training Board, 8 The Arndale Centre, Luton, LU1 2TS, or from any local council.

A ten-week tree surgery course is available at Merrist Wood Agricultural College, Worplesdon, near Guildford, Surrey. This course is designed for those with proven tree-climbing ability employed in local authorities or commercial companies and covers all aspects of tree surgery at craft level. The course terminates with the City & Guilds of London Institute Special Examination for Craftsmen in Tree Surgery.

A more general arboricultural course for craftsmen leading to a City & Guilds Stage II Certificate in Arboriculture is available at the Cheshire

College of Agriculture, Reaseheath, Nantwich, Cheshire. This course has six two-week college blocks over two years.

The one-year course in arboriculture offered at Merrist Wood Agricultural College is a comprehensive 35-week full-time course covering all aspects of arboriculture. Depending on their previous experience students can, on completion of the course, enter the industry at various levels.

Supervisors

Progression from craftsman to foreman or supervisor is normally on ability and ambition. Supervisory skills, however, need careful and thorough training. A number of supervisory courses are offered through the industrial and local government training boards and education centres, some leading to the National Examination Board for Supervisory Studies examinations.

A three-week tree surgery course for foremen designed for experienced tree surgeons is available at Merrist Wood Agricultural College. This course leads to the City & Guilds Special Examination for Foremen in Tree Surgery.

A three-year ordinary national diploma course in arboriculture is designed for those with a minimum of one year's practical experience and at least four approved 'O' levels or equivalent. The first college year, the middle industrial sandwich year and the third college year take the student through craft and supervisory skills and prepare him for a career in arboriculture; on ability, he can progress to higher positions. The first and third college years are covered at Merrist Wood and the pre-entry and sandwich years in suitable industrial employment.

Managerial staff

The ability to organise and manage arboricultural features, equipment and staff efficiency requires considerable experience and can be aided or improved by education. Some of the schemes already mentioned, particularly the Ordinary National Diploma course, cover supervisory and managerial skills and responsibilities. The training boards offer a range of managerial courses, as do a number of educational establishments.

Technologists

The scientific and technological expertise required for arboriculture is covered at this time by graduates from horticulture and forestry. In the future, particularly when arboricultural research becomes properly organised and financed, there will be a need for technologists specialising in arboriculture. Post-graduate courses or even BSc degree courses should be available in the not-too-distant future.

Royal Forestry Society Arboricultural Examinations

The Royal Forestry Society of England, Wales and Northern Ireland instituted specific examinations in Arboriculture – in 1958 the Certificate and in 1959 the Diploma in Arboriculture (later to be called the National Diploma in Arboriculture). Candidates for the Certificate examination must be over eighteen years of age and to progress to the National Diploma must hold the Certificate and must have proven ability in handling tree-work machinery. Further details of the syllabus and fees can be obtained from the Secretary, Royal Forestry Society, 102 High Street, Tring, Herts. A number of day release, evening, correspondence and short block courses are available throughout the country to help prepare for these examinations.

Arboricultural Education for Allied Professions

Many staff of allied industries and professions require a knowledge of trees as part of their duties. This applies particularly to landscape architects, horticulturists, planners and national and county parks staff. Many of the educational schemes for these staff do include arboriculture but often in insufficient detail to give the students a working knowledge.

Short block release courses can be made available for those staff who require further knowledge. Courses in Amenity Woodland and Forestry are available at the Cumbria College of Agriculture, Newton Rigg, Penrith, and a one-week course in Arboriculture for Planning Officers at Merrist Wood.

A 24-week supplementary course in arboriculture has been planned at Merrist Wood Arboricultural College designed specifically for those who have completed an OND course or equivalent in an allied subject.

Careers Advice

Proper advice is essential if staff are to make full use of the further education and training schemes that are available. School-leavers can seek advice from careers teachers, the Youth Employment Service or from the County Agricultural Education Adviser.

The Department of Education and Science produces a booklet, *Agricultural Education*, which gives details of all full-time and sandwich courses in agriculture, horticulture, forestry and arboriculture in England and Wales. This is available from the Education Officer, Department of Education and Science, Elizabeth House, York Road, London, SE1.

The Arboricultural Association produces a leaflet, *Careers in Arboriculture*, which advises on career prospects and educational and training courses available in arboriculture. It is obtainable from the Secretary, c/o Merrist Wood Agricultural College, Worplesdon, Guildford, Surrey, GU3 3PE.

Acknowledgements

The author acknowledges with thanks the assistance of colleagues at Merrist Wood Agricultural College, in particular Mrs Pamela Jordan, Mr Derek Patch, and Mr M. John Whitehead for his artwork and photographs.

He also wishes to thank Mr Michael Neale (for plates 23, 35, 42 and 43), Bridon Fibres and Plastics Ltd for their advice on the section on ropes in Chapter 4, Omark International Ltd and Danarm Ltd for their advice on the chain saw section in the same chapter, and Mrs Leonie Bridgeman for her consideration and help in preparing the manuscript.

P.H.B.

Index

public, safety of, 27-9, 90, 116, 122

quick-rotting wood, 57-8

rakes, 42
reduction and shaping, 67-74
regrowth, unwanted, 74, *70, 71, 72*
remedial surgery, 90-115, 136
respiration, 10, 15
restoration, 74
retaining wall, 74, *73*
road signs, 29
rod bracing, 87, 102
roots, 14-15, 131, 132; damage by, 16, 134;
    pruning, 15, 74; *see also* feeding
ropes, 31-7
Royal Forestry Society examinations, 9, 137, 139

safety, 19, 20-30, 58, 122(2); of property, 29-30;
    of public, 27-9, 90, 116, 122; regulations, 20,
    30
Santar, 54
sapwood, 12, 14, *13*
saw, chain, 22, 46-52, *44, 45, 61;* hand, 40, *38, 39*
scaffolding, 39
screw-eye, 80-4, *81*
sealants, wound, 54, 55, 64, 90
seasons for tree work, 57, 122
secateurs, 42, *41*
secondary thickening, 12
services, public, *see* telephone lines; underground
    services
set, on saws, 40
seven drawn strand cable, 75-80
sink, sink cut, 118, *117, 119*
sisal ropes, 31, 32
slashers, 40-2
slinging, of branches, 63
snatching, 119
sodium chlorate, 55, 120
soil, 15, 112; alteration to soil/site levels, 74, 131,
    132, 136
specifications, contract, 121-3
splicing, 34, *35*
sprayers, 52
standing Committee on Arboricultural Education,
    9, 137
stem, *see* trunk and branch systems
storage , of equipment, 34-7, 39, 40, 53
storm damage, 110
street trees, 18-19, 74, 125
strops, 24
stump disposal, 120; stump-cutters, 52-3, 120;
    stump killing, 55, 120

sub-contractors, 122
supervision, of site work, 29, 122, 123, 135
surveys, 125-7; *see also* inspection

teamwork, 21
telephone lines, 30, 122
tensioning, of cables, 83, 84-5, *79*
terylene ropes, 31, 32
test-boring, 130
thimbles, 83, *81*
tie-rod, 87, 102, *84, 85, 86*
timber hitch, 32, 34, *33*
Tirfor winches, 44, *43*
tolerance, of trees, to site works, 136
tools, 27, 39-53, 83, 95, 122, *38, 41, 44, 45, 49,*
    50, 97, 98
Town & Country Amenities Act (1974), 18
Town & Country Planning Acts, 17
traffic warning and control, 29, 122, *62*
training, *see* education and training
transpiration, 10-12, 14-15, 56
transport, vehicles, 19, 53
Tree Council, 9
Trewhella 'Monkey' winch, 43-4, *42*
trunk and branch systems, 12-14, 130, *13*

U clip, *see* bulldog-grips
underground services, 30, 122
Urethane foam filler, 55

vandalism, 90
vehicles, transport, 19, 53
vertigo, 20
vibration, from chain saws, 22
visors, 22

water loss, 12
water pockets, 110, *111*
water table, waterlogging, 15, 132
weather, 21
weight, of branches, 32
whipping, of ropes, 34, *35*
white-finger disease, 22
wildlife, conservation of, 8
winches, 43-6, 116-17, 120, *42, 43*
wire mesh, 55
wire ropes, *see* cables
wood formation, 12-14
woodpeckers, 95
workshop, 53
wound sealants, 54, 55, 64, 90

Xylamon Arbor, 55
xylem, 12, *13*